Robinson, Alex
ISBN: 1-891830-46-5
1. Graphic novels
2. Fiction

BOP!
September 2003. All
contents © 2003 Alex Robinson, except "Cartoonist's Widow" ©
2003 Kristen Siebecker and Alex Robinson. Edited by Chris Staros. Art direction and
design by Brett Warnock. Proofreading by Robert
Venditti. Published by Top Shelf Productions, Brett
Warnock and Chris Staros, PO Box 1282, Marietta,
GA, 30061-1282. Top Shelf Productions and the Top
Shelf logo are ® and © 2003 Top Shelf Productions,
Inc. The stories, characters, and incidents featured
in this publication are entirely fictional. No part of
this book may be reproduced without permis-
sion, except small excerpts for purposes
of review. Check out our website at
www.topshelfcomix.com
Please visit Alex Robinson's website
http://members.aol.com/ComicBookAlex

Printed in Canada

Introduction
by John Kovalic

"Alex Robinson is a genius and everyone on Earth should kneel before him and give him awards and junk and throw lots of money his way and stuff." That, I believe, is what Alex Robinson's publisher (perhaps even Alex himself) might want me to say in an introduction to this, a collection of amazing "Box Office Poison" stories. Perhaps not in so many words, but there you go. Which isn't to say it's not true. When I was thinking of turning *Dork Tower* into a full-fledged comic book, I visited my local comic shop for the first time in ten years (the late '80's and early '90's drove me—and about ten million other people—away from the hobby). Just to see what black & white indy comics were out there, you understand.

Among many forgettable books that I grabbed in the name of Tax Deductible Market Research were a few gems. One, called *Box Office Poison*, had an intriguing title and really cool art. So I read it first. And I was hooked. The sardonic humor, the poignant, wistful narrative and the utter humanity behind these stories are hard not to be hooked by. Sherman, Ed, Jane, Dorothy, et al., aren't simply characters you grow to know—they're characters you already know. These are your friends and family; these are people whose lives don't have tidy beginnings and neat, pat endings. They are people with petty everyday worries and troubles, and Alex's ability to spin these into sometime sad, sometimes quirky, sometimes side-splitting stories is sheer magic. That's when I realized Alex Robinson is a genius and everyone on Earth should kneel before him and give him awards and junk, and throw lots of money his way and stuff.

So now for something Alex probably didn't want me to say... He's a jolly guy. I consider myself deeply fortunate to be able to call Alex a friend. Yet if there's one thing I've learned over the years we've known each other, it's that the fellow behind the dark, angsty genius of *Box Office Poison* is a hoot. A riot. Jolly, even. He's a good chum to drink far into the night with, to joke with, to swap stories with, and to share petty, everyday worries and troubles with. Which may be part of the reason *Box Office Poison* rings so true: Alex isn't just a great storyteller, he's a great listener, and a great observer. He cares about (in the words of REM) life and how to live it, as is apparent in almost every page of *Box Office Poison*.

So (as I believe we've already established) everyone on Earth should kneel before him and give him awards and junk and throw lots of money his way and stuff. Not just because *Box Office Poison* rocks (It does! It does!), but also because Alex is simply one of the coolest, most thoughtful, and genuinely honest people in this biz. Plus, he's jolly. And we need that. Seriously.

Madison, WI, April 13, 2003

(In a never ending effort to become a millionaire, John Kovalic is a publisher, a political cartoonist, an illustrator, and a gaming mogul. He is most famous, however, for his funny, award winning comic book *Dork Tower*. For more information on this Wisconsin based Renaissance man, check out his website www.dorktower.com.)

BOP !

[More Box Office Poison]

By Alex Robinson

"In Which TV Show Would You Live?", **Who Should be Shot at Dawn?**, "Who Will Play You in the Inevitable *Box Office Poison* Movie?", **What Would You Change Your Name To?**, and "Which Celebrity Will You Be Sleeping With?" originally appeared in the serialized comic book *Box Office Poison* published by Antarctic Press, 1996-2000.

"Temptation" originally appeared in full color in the *Box Office Poison Kolor Karnival* published by Antarctic Press, 1999.

"Jane's High School Reunion" originally appeared in the *SPX 1997* anthology.

"Grudge" originally appeared in the *SPX 1998* anthology.

"King Horse" originally appeared in the *Expo 2000* anthology.

"My Old Flame, or Ex-Man" originally appeared in *Private Beach* #4, published by Slave Labor Graphics in 2002.

"Box Office Poison 2000" originally appeared in the *Expo 1999* anthology.

"Cartoonist's Widow" originally appeared in the *Expo 2001* anthology.

"Flat Earth" originally appeared in *Brilliant Mistake* #1. It was started at 11:20 a.m. on 1 April 2002 and completed at 10:25 a.m. on 2 April 2002.

"Caprice" is an excerpt from *Tricked*, to be published in 2004 by Top Shelf Productions, assuming Alex gets off his lazy ass and starts producing.

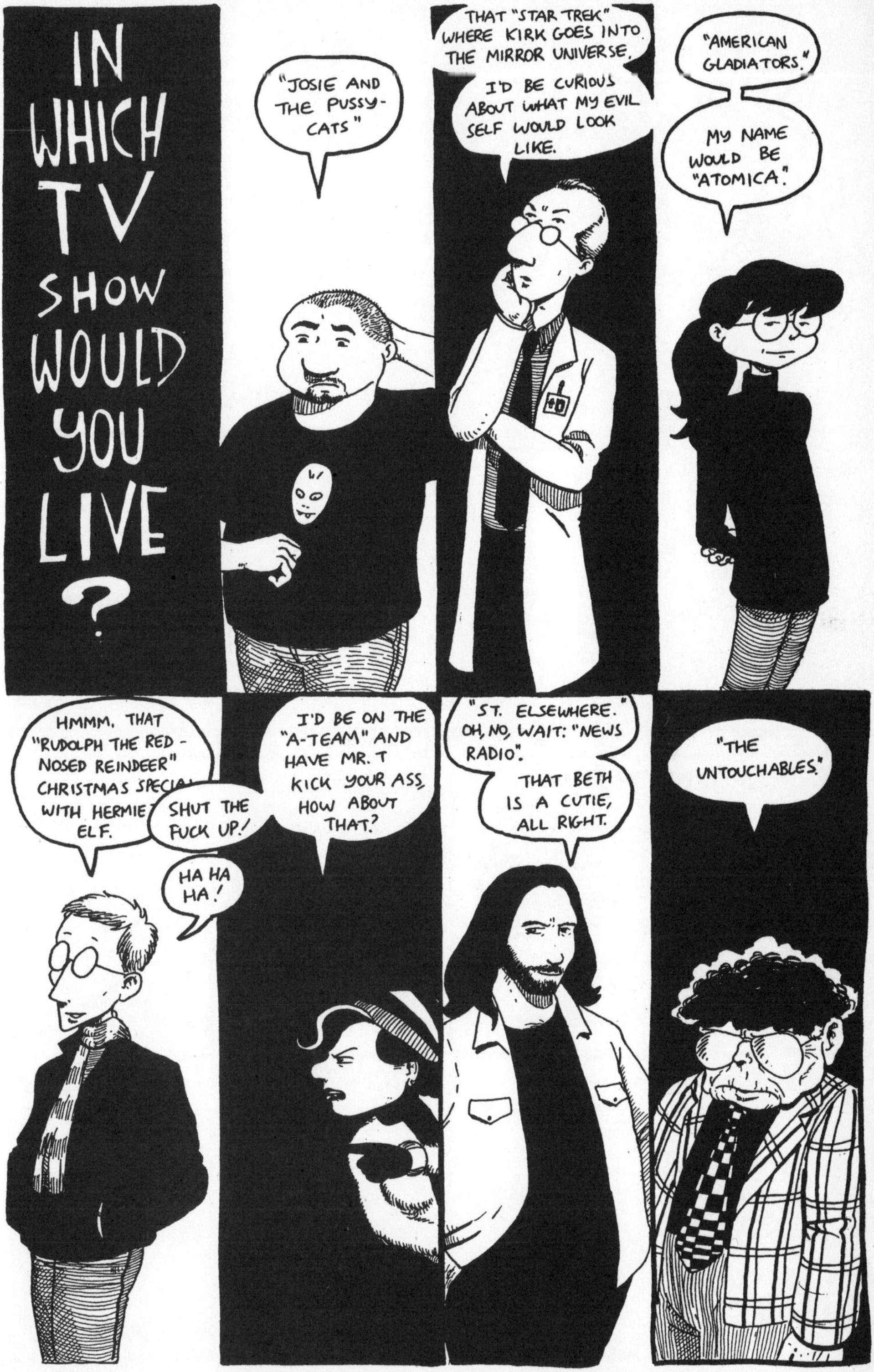

IN WHICH TV SHOW WOULD YOU LIVE?
"JOSIE AND THE PUSSY-CATS"
THAT "STAR TREK" WHERE KIRK GOES INTO THE MIRROR UNIVERSE.
I'D BE CURIOUS ABOUT WHAT MY EVIL SELF WOULD LOOK LIKE.
"AMERICAN GLADIATORS."
MY NAME WOULD BE "ATOMICA".
HMMM. THAT "RUDOLPH THE RED-NOSED REINDEER" CHRISTMAS SPECIA WITH HERMIE ELF.
SHUT THE FUCK UP!
HA HA HA!
I'D BE ON THE "A-TEAM" AND HAVE MR. T KICK YOUR ASS, HOW ABOUT THAT?
"ST. ELSEWHERE." OH, NO, WAIT: "NEWS RADIO".
THAT BETH IS A CUTIE, ALL RIGHT.
"THE UNTOUCHABLES."

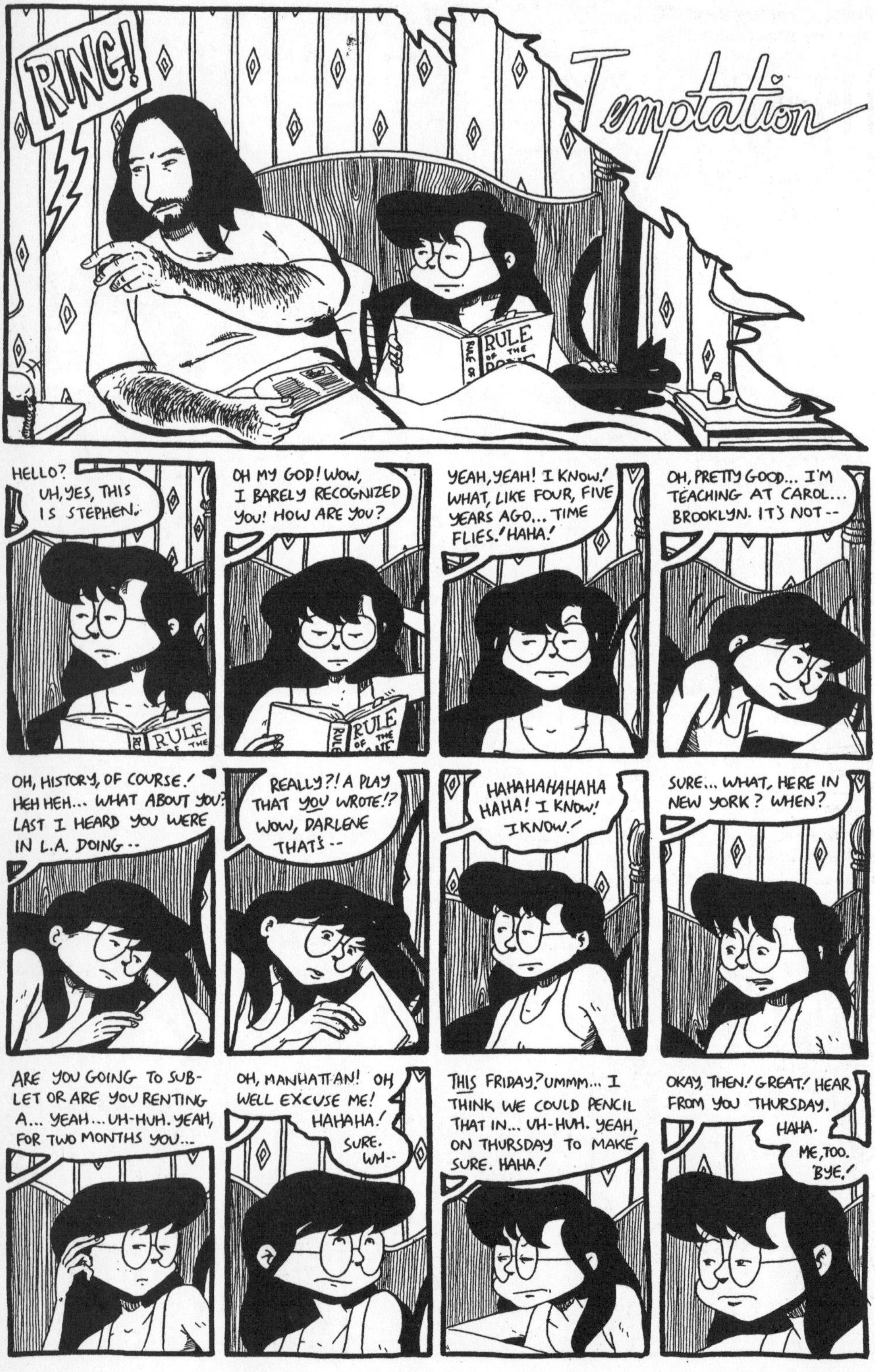

RING!
Temptation
HELLO? UH, YES, THIS IS STEPHEN.
OH MY GOD! WOW, I BARELY RECOGNIZED YOU! HOW ARE YOU?
YEAH, YEAH! I KNOW! WHAT, LIKE FOUR, FIVE YEARS AGO... TIME FLIES! HAHA!
OH, PRETTY GOOD... I'M TEACHING AT CAROL... BROOKLYN. IT'S NOT--
OH, HISTORY, OF COURSE! HEH HEH... WHAT ABOUT YOU? LAST I HEARD YOU WERE IN L.A. DOING--
REALLY?! A PLAY THAT YOU WROTE!? WOW, DARLENE THAT'S--
HAHAHAHAHAHA HAHA! I KNOW! I KNOW!
SURE... WHAT, HERE IN NEW YORK? WHEN?
ARE YOU GOING TO SUB-LET OR ARE YOU RENTING A... YEAH... UH-HUH. YEAH, FOR TWO MONTHS YOU...
OH, MANHATTAN! OH WELL EXCUSE ME! HAHAHA! SURE. WH--
THIS FRIDAY? UMMM... I THINK WE COULD PENCIL THAT IN... UH-HUH. YEAH, ON THURSDAY TO MAKE SURE. HAHA!
OKAY, THEN! GREAT! HEAR FROM YOU THURSDAY. HAHA. ME, TOO. BYE!

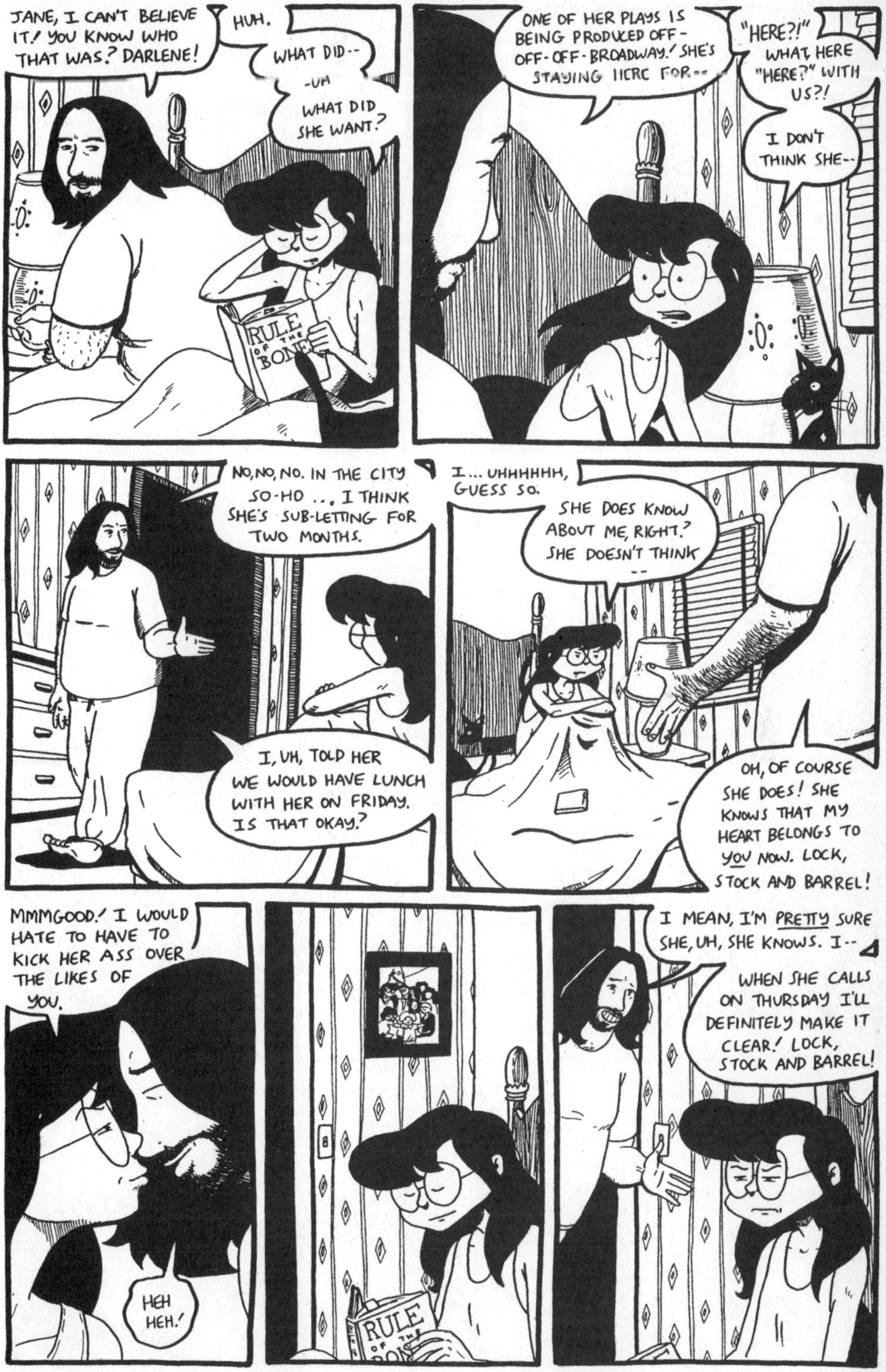
JANE, I CAN'T BELIEVE IT! YOU KNOW WHO THAT WAS? DARLENE!
HUH.
WHAT DID--
-UH
WHAT DID SHE WANT?
ONE OF HER PLAYS IS BEING PRODUCED OFF-OFF-OFF-BROADWAY! SHE'S STAYING HERE FOR--
"HERE?!"
WHAT, HERE "HERE?" WITH US?!
I DON'T THINK SHE--
NO, NO, NO. IN THE CITY SO-HO ..., I THINK SHE'S SUB-LETTING FOR TWO MONTHS.
I, UH, TOLD HER WE WOULD HAVE LUNCH WITH HER ON FRIDAY. IS THAT OKAY?
I... UHHHHHH, GUESS SO.
SHE DOES KNOW ABOUT ME, RIGHT? SHE DOESN'T THINK --
OH, OF COURSE SHE DOES! SHE KNOWS THAT MY HEART BELONGS TO YOU NOW. LOCK, STOCK AND BARREL!
MMMGOOD! I WOULD HATE TO HAVE TO KICK HER ASS OVER THE LIKES OF YOU.
HEH HEH!
RULE OF THE BONE
I MEAN, I'M PRETTY SURE SHE, UH, SHE KNOWS. I--
WHEN SHE CALLS ON THURSDAY I'LL DEFINITELY MAKE IT CLEAR! LOCK, STOCK AND BARREL!

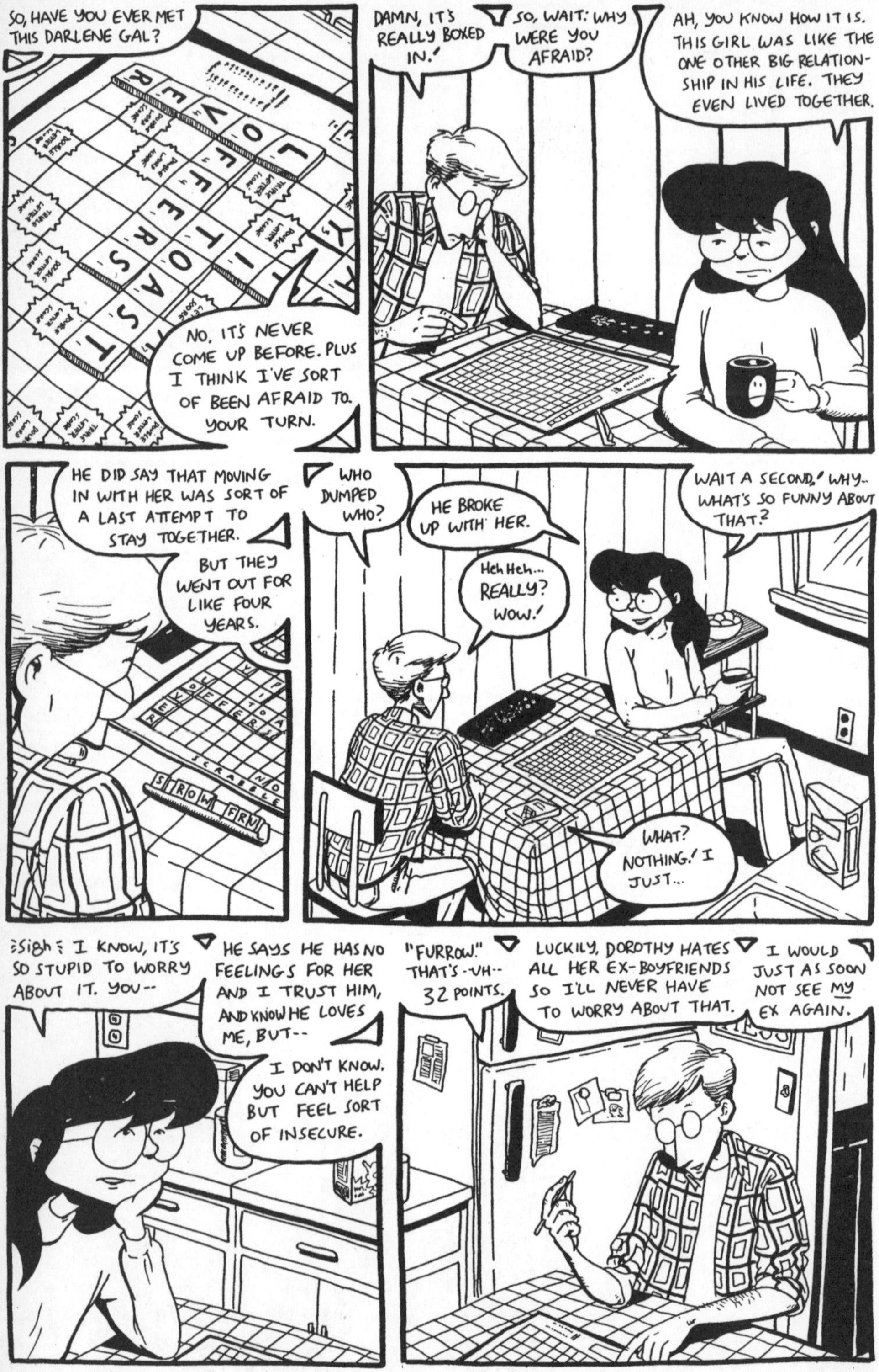
SO, HAVE YOU EVER MET THIS DARLENE GAL?
NO. IT'S NEVER COME UP BEFORE. PLUS I THINK I'VE SORT OF BEEN AFRAID TO. YOUR TURN.
DAMN, IT'S REALLY BOXED IN.!
SO, WAIT: WHY WERE YOU AFRAID?
AH, YOU KNOW HOW IT IS. THIS GIRL WAS LIKE THE ONE OTHER BIG RELATIONSHIP IN HIS LIFE. THEY EVEN LIVED TOGETHER.
HE DID SAY THAT MOVING IN WITH HER WAS SORT OF A LAST ATTEMPT TO STAY TOGETHER.
BUT THEY WENT OUT FOR LIKE FOUR YEARS.
WHO DUMPED WHO?
HE BROKE UP WITH HER.
Heh Heh... REALLY? WOW.!
WAIT A SECOND.! WHY.. WHAT'S SO FUNNY ABOUT THAT?
WHAT? NOTHING.! I JUST...
≷Sigh≷ I KNOW, IT'S SO STUPID TO WORRY ABOUT IT. YOU--
HE SAYS HE HAS NO FEELINGS FOR HER AND I TRUST HIM, AND KNOW HE LOVES ME, BUT--
I DON'T KNOW. YOU CAN'T HELP BUT FEEL SORT OF INSECURE.
"FURROW." THAT'S --UH-- 32 POINTS.
LUCKILY, DOROTHY HATES ALL HER EX-BOYFRIENDS SO I'LL NEVER HAVE TO WORRY ABOUT THAT.
I WOULD JUST AS SOON NOT SEE MY EX AGAIN.

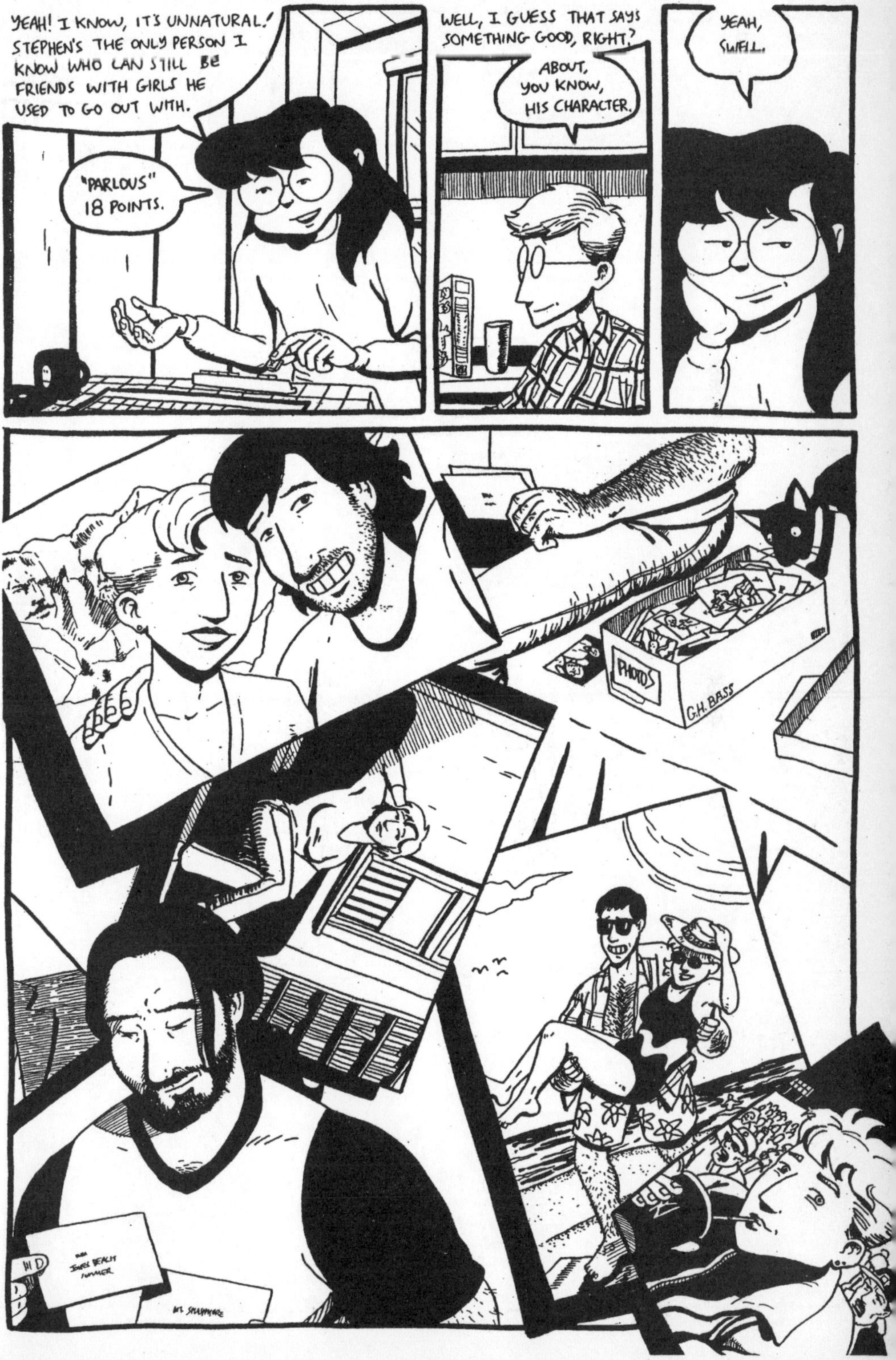
YEAH! I KNOW, IT'S UNNATURAL! STEPHEN'S THE ONLY PERSON I KNOW WHO CAN STILL BE FRIENDS WITH GIRLS HE USED TO GO OUT WITH.
"PARLOUS" 18 POINTS.
WELL, I GUESS THAT SAYS SOMETHING GOOD, RIGHT?
ABOUT, YOU KNOW, HIS CHARACTER.
YEAH, SWELL.
PHOTOS
G.H. BASS

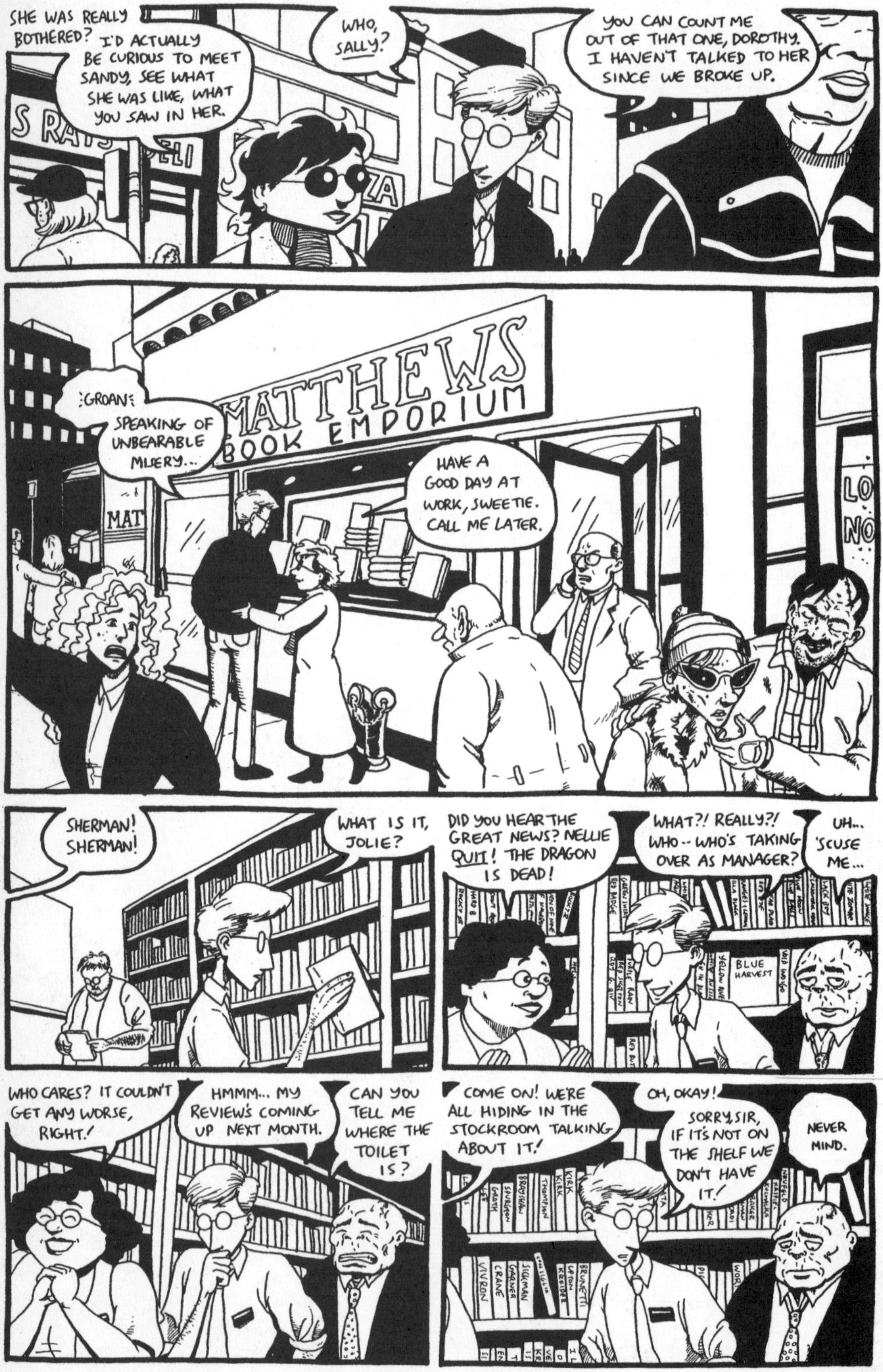

SHE WAS REALLY BOTHERED?
I'D ACTUALLY BE CURIOUS TO MEET SANDY, SEE WHAT SHE WAS LIKE, WHAT YOU SAW IN HER.
WHO, SALLY?
YOU CAN COUNT ME OUT OF THAT ONE, DOROTHY. I HAVEN'T TALKED TO HER SINCE WE BROKE UP.
MATTHEWS BOOK EMPORIUM
:GROAN:
SPEAKING OF UNBEARABLE MISERY...
HAVE A GOOD DAY AT WORK, SWEETIE. CALL ME LATER.
SHERMAN! SHERMAN!
WHAT IS IT, JOLIE?
DID YOU HEAR THE GREAT NEWS? NELLIE QUIT! THE DRAGON IS DEAD!
WHAT?! REALLY?! WHO -- WHO'S TAKING OVER AS MANAGER?
UH... 'SCUSE ME...
BLUE HARVEST
WHO CARES? IT COULDN'T GET ANY WORSE, RIGHT!
HMMM... MY REVIEW'S COMING UP NEXT MONTH.
CAN YOU TELL ME WHERE THE TOILET IS?
COME ON! WE'RE ALL HIDING IN THE STOCKROOM TALKING ABOUT IT!
OH, OKAY!
SORRY, SIR, IF IT'S NOT ON THE SHELF WE DON'T HAVE IT!
NEVER MIND.

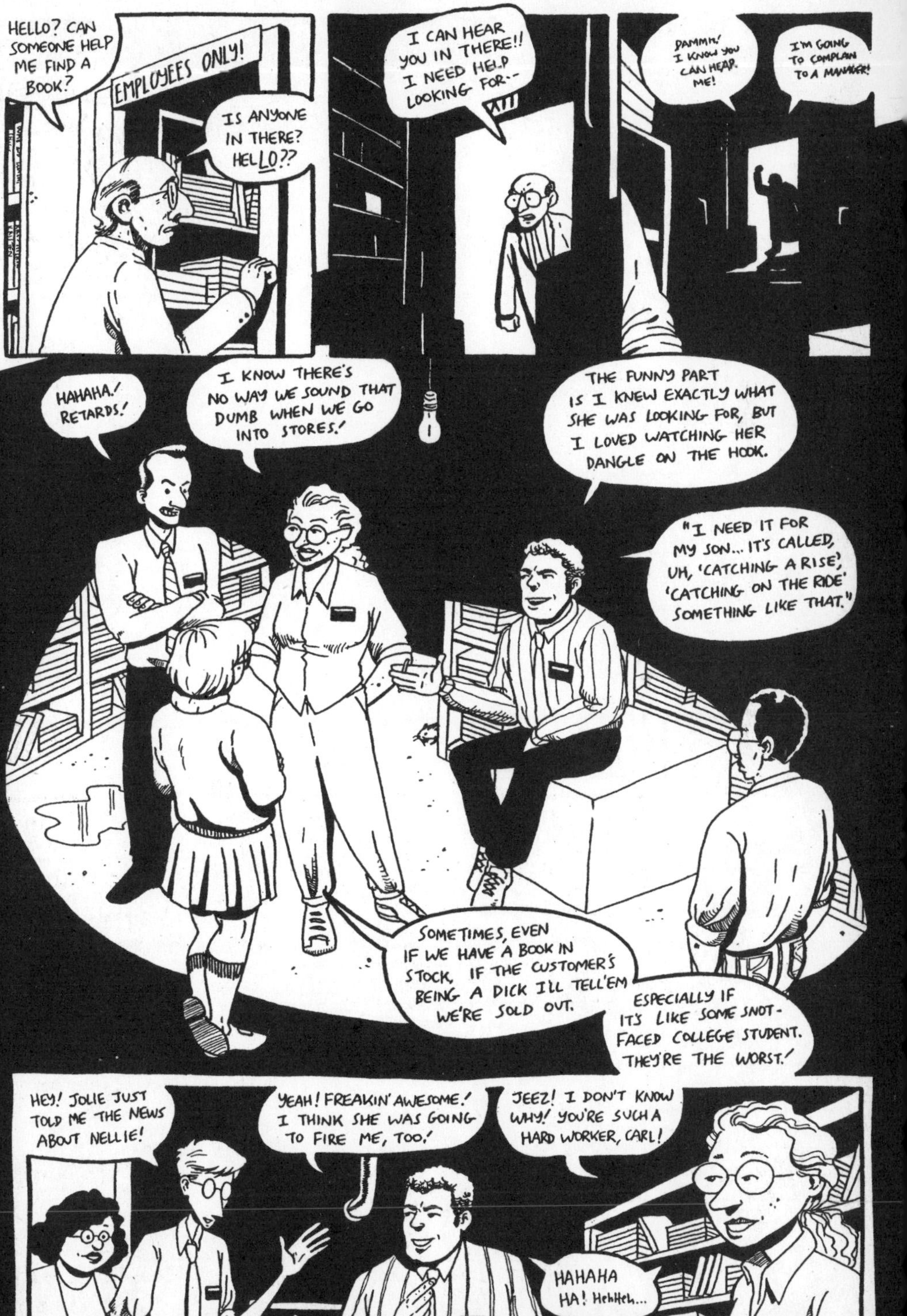
HELLO? CAN SOMEONE HELP ME FIND A BOOK?
EMPLOYEES ONLY!
IS ANYONE IN THERE? HELLO??
I CAN HEAR YOU IN THERE!! I NEED HELP LOOKING FOR--
DAMMIT! I KNOW YOU CAN HEAR ME!
I'M GOING TO COMPLAIN TO A MANAGER!
HAHAHA! RETARDS!
I KNOW THERE'S NO WAY WE SOUND THAT DUMB WHEN WE GO INTO STORES!
THE FUNNY PART IS I KNEW EXACTLY WHAT SHE WAS LOOKING FOR, BUT I LOVED WATCHING HER DANGLE ON THE HOOK.
"I NEED IT FOR MY SON... IT'S CALLED, UH, 'CATCHING A RISE', 'CATCHING ON THE RIDE' SOMETHING LIKE THAT."
SOMETIMES, EVEN IF WE HAVE A BOOK IN STOCK, IF THE CUSTOMER'S BEING A DICK I'LL TELL'EM WE'RE SOLD OUT.
ESPECIALLY IF IT'S LIKE SOME SNOT-FACED COLLEGE STUDENT. THEY'RE THE WORST!
HEY! JOLIE JUST TOLD ME THE NEWS ABOUT NELLIE!
YEAH! FREAKIN' AWESOME! I THINK SHE WAS GOING TO FIRE ME, TOO!
JEEZ! I DON'T KNOW WHY! YOU'RE SUCH A HARD WORKER, CARL!
HAHAHA HA! HehHeh...

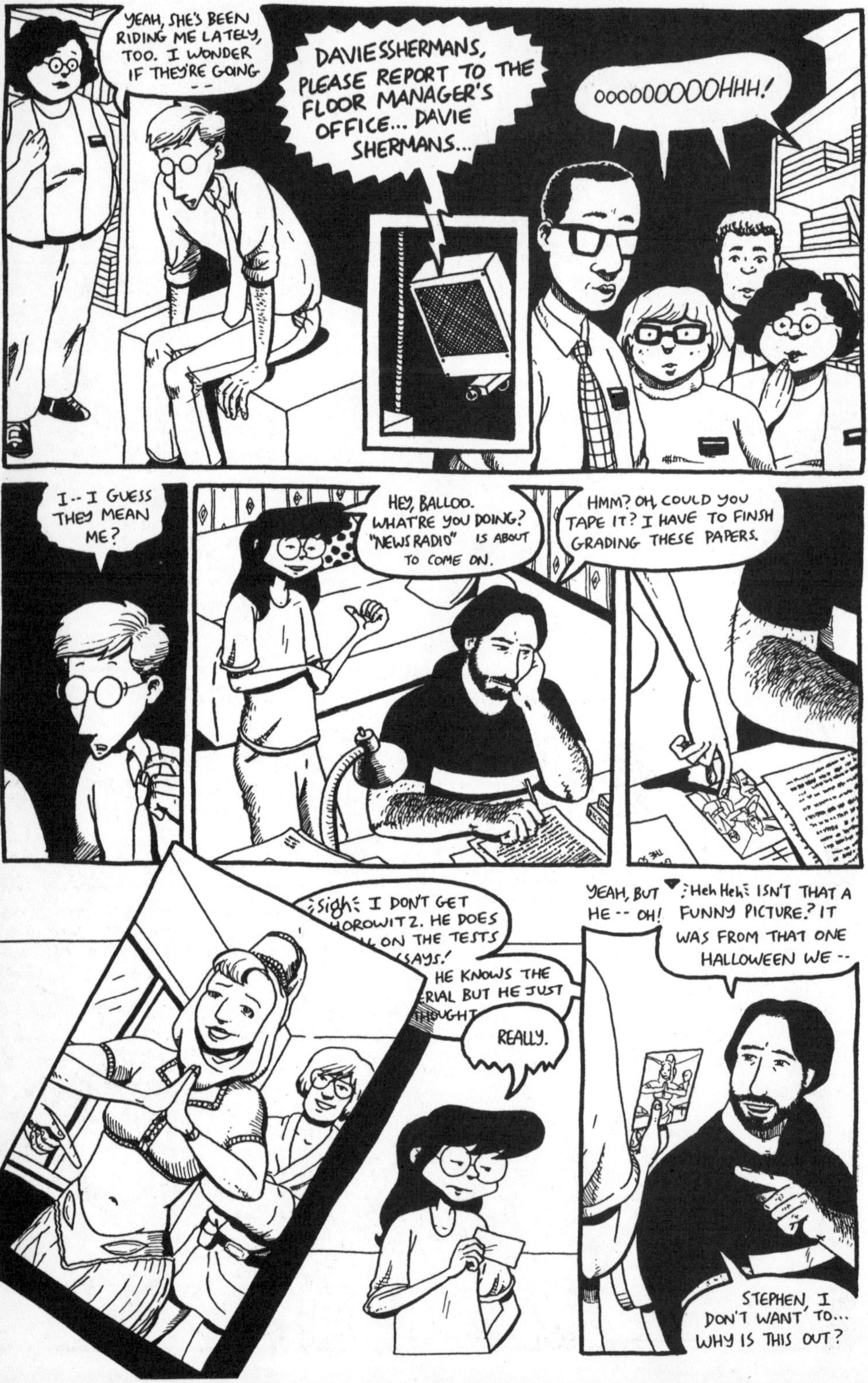
YEAH, SHE'S BEEN RIDING ME LATELY, TOO. I WONDER IF THEY'RE GOING --
DAVIESSHERMANS, PLEASE REPORT TO THE FLOOR MANAGER'S OFFICE... DAVIE SHERMANS...
OOOOOOOOOHHH!
I-- I GUESS THEY MEAN ME?
HEY, BALLOO. WHAT'RE YOU DOING? "NEWS RADIO" IS ABOUT TO COME ON.
HMM? OH, COULD YOU TAPE IT? I HAVE TO FINSH GRADING THESE PAPERS.
Sigh I DON'T GET
HE DOES
ON THE TESTS
HE KNOWS THE
BUT HE JUST
REALLY.
YEAH, BUT HE -- OH!
Heh Heh ISN'T THAT A FUNNY PICTURE? IT WAS FROM THAT ONE HALLOWEEN WE --
STEPHEN, I DON'T WANT TO... WHY IS THIS OUT?

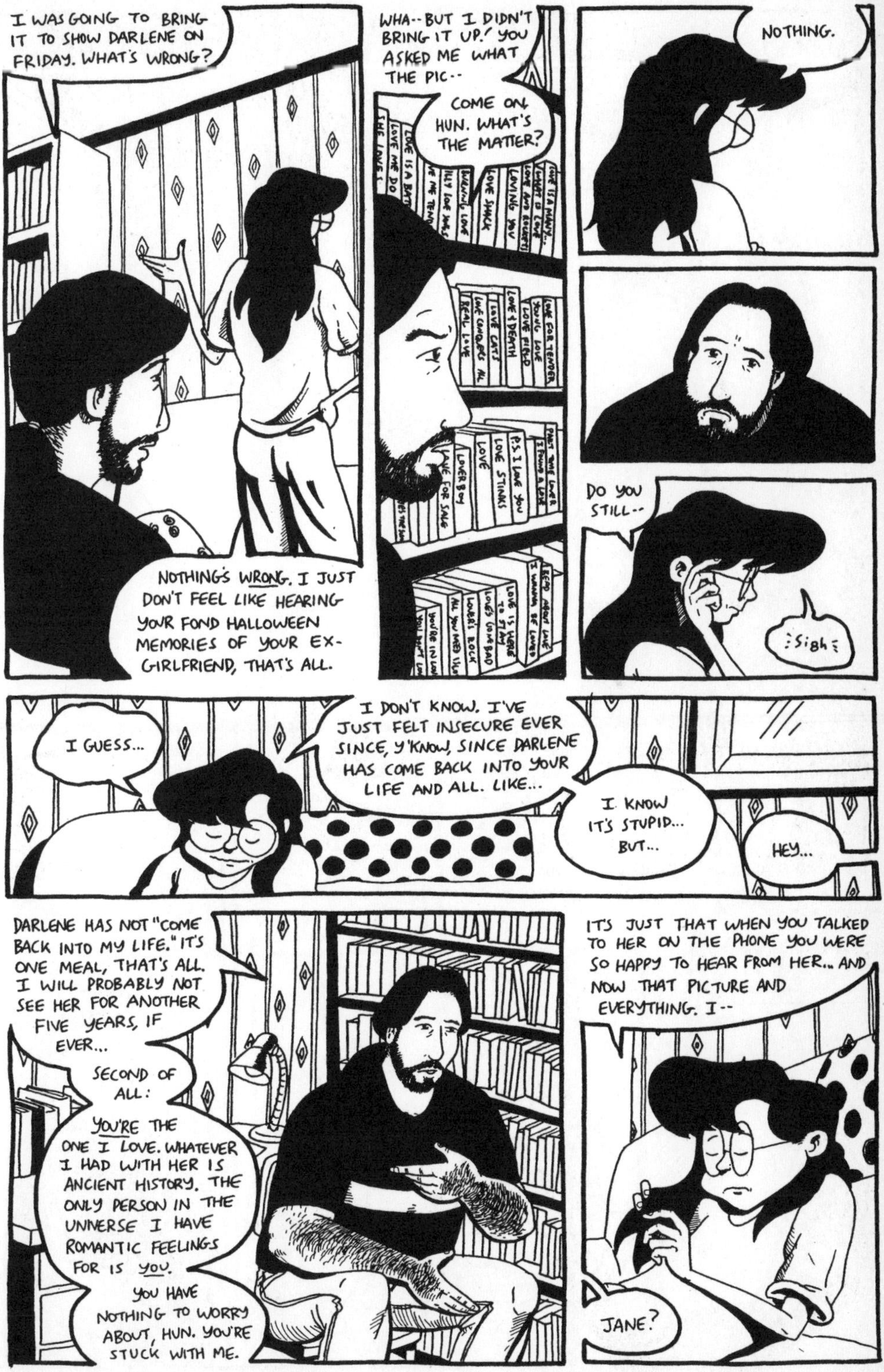

I WAS GOING TO BRING IT TO SHOW DARLENE ON FRIDAY. WHAT'S WRONG?
NOTHING'S WRONG. I JUST DON'T FEEL LIKE HEARING YOUR FOND HALLOWEEN MEMORIES OF YOUR EX-GIRLFRIEND, THAT'S ALL.
WHA-- BUT I DIDN'T BRING IT UP! YOU ASKED ME WHAT THE PIC--
COME ON, HUN. WHAT'S THE MATTER?
NOTHING.
DO YOU STILL--
SIGH
I GUESS...
I DON'T KNOW. I'VE JUST FELT INSECURE EVER SINCE, Y'KNOW, SINCE DARLENE HAS COME BACK INTO YOUR LIFE AND ALL. LIKE...
I KNOW IT'S STUPID... BUT...
HEY...
DARLENE HAS NOT "COME BACK INTO MY LIFE." IT'S ONE MEAL, THAT'S ALL. I WILL PROBABLY NOT SEE HER FOR ANOTHER FIVE YEARS, IF EVER...
SECOND OF ALL:
YOU'RE THE ONE I LOVE. WHATEVER I HAD WITH HER IS ANCIENT HISTORY. THE ONLY PERSON IN THE UNIVERSE I HAVE ROMANTIC FEELINGS FOR IS YOU.
YOU HAVE NOTHING TO WORRY ABOUT, HUN. YOU'RE STUCK WITH ME.
IT'S JUST THAT WHEN YOU TALKED TO HER ON THE PHONE YOU WERE SO HAPPY TO HEAR FROM HER... AND NOW THAT PICTURE AND EVERYTHING. I--
JANE?

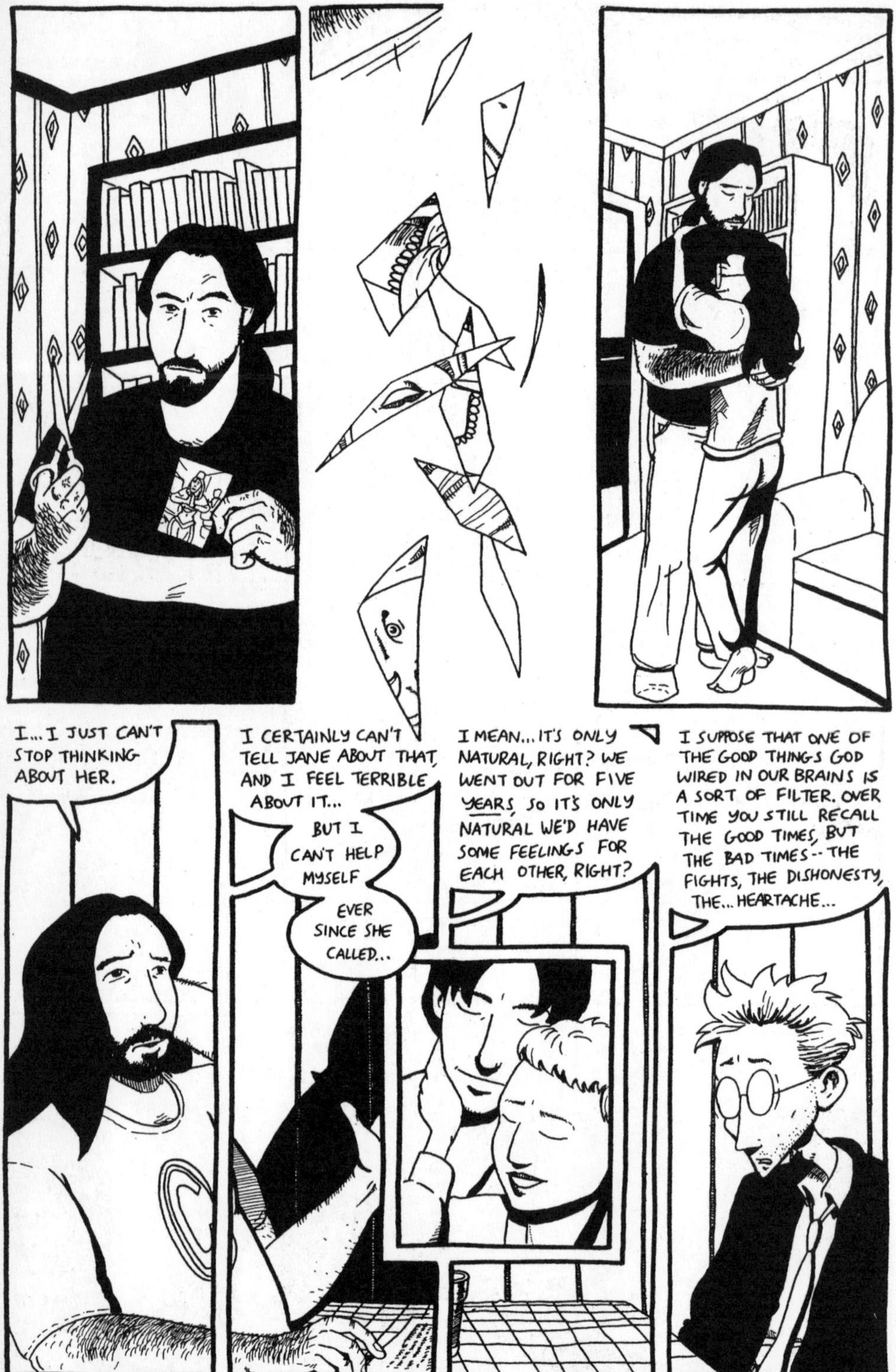
I... I JUST CAN'T STOP THINKING ABOUT HER.
I CERTAINLY CAN'T TELL JANE ABOUT THAT, AND I FEEL TERRIBLE ABOUT IT...
BUT I CAN'T HELP MYSELF
EVER SINCE SHE CALLED...
I MEAN... IT'S ONLY NATURAL, RIGHT? WE WENT OUT FOR FIVE YEARS, SO IT'S ONLY NATURAL WE'D HAVE SOME FEELINGS FOR EACH OTHER, RIGHT?
I SUPPOSE THAT ONE OF THE GOOD THINGS GOD WIRED IN OUR BRAINS IS A SORT OF FILTER. OVER TIME YOU STILL RECALL THE GOOD TIMES, BUT THE BAD TIMES -- THE FIGHTS, THE DISHONESTY, THE... HEARTACHE...

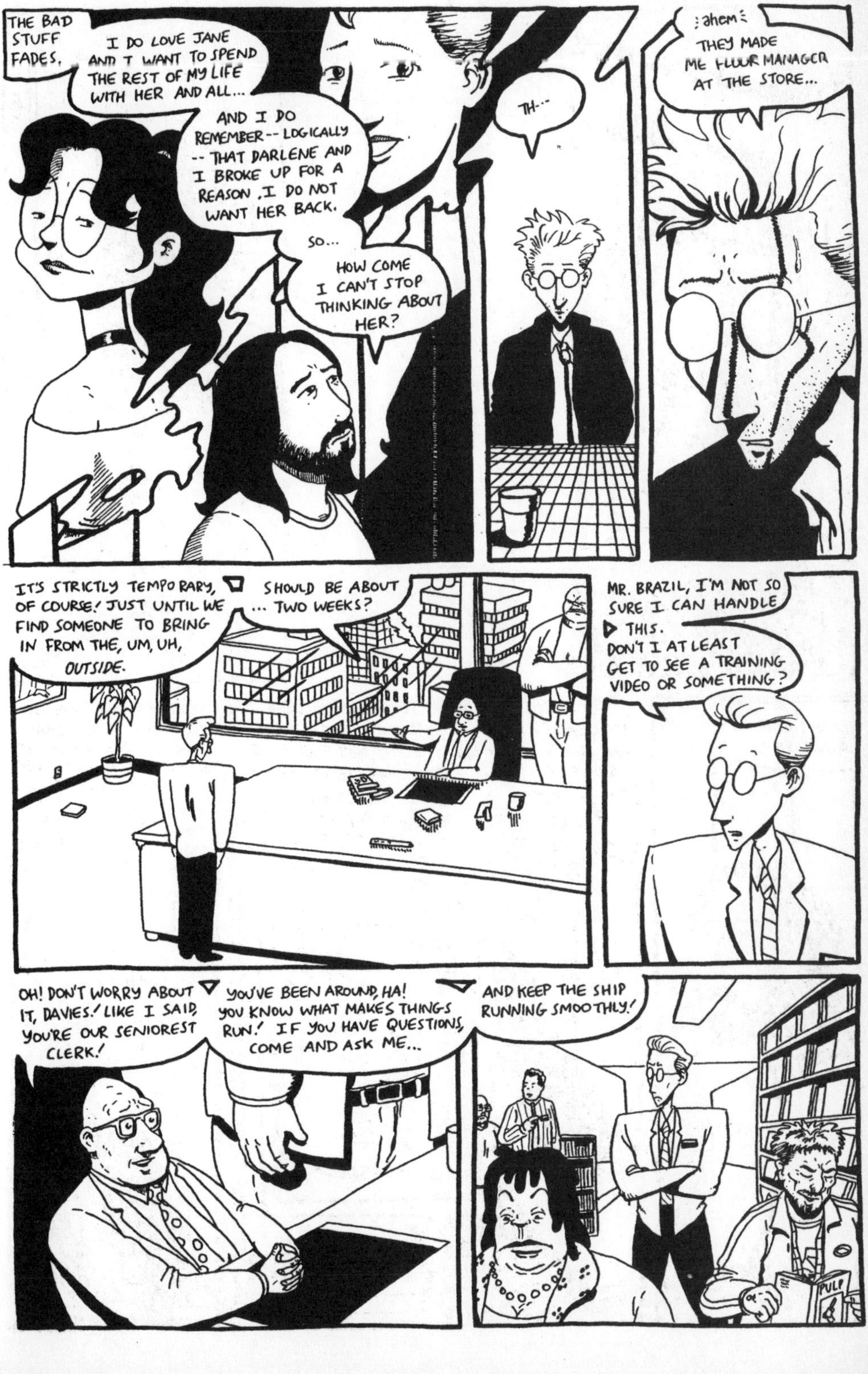
THE BAD STUFF FADES.
I DO LOVE JANE AND I WANT TO SPEND THE REST OF MY LIFE WITH HER AND ALL...
AND I DO REMEMBER -- LOGICALLY -- THAT DARLENE AND I BROKE UP FOR A REASON. I DO NOT WANT HER BACK.
SO...
HOW COME I CAN'T STOP THINKING ABOUT HER?
TH--
:ahem:
THEY MADE ME FLOOR MANAGER AT THE STORE...
IT'S STRICTLY TEMPORARY, OF COURSE! JUST UNTIL WE FIND SOMEONE TO BRING IN FROM THE, UM, UH, OUTSIDE.
SHOULD BE ABOUT ... TWO WEEKS?
MR. BRAZIL, I'M NOT SO SURE I CAN HANDLE THIS.
DON'T I AT LEAST GET TO SEE A TRAINING VIDEO OR SOMETHING?
OH! DON'T WORRY ABOUT IT, DAVIES! LIKE I SAID, YOU'RE OUR SENIOREST CLERK!
YOU'VE BEEN AROUND, HA! YOU KNOW WHAT MAKES THINGS RUN! IF YOU HAVE QUESTIONS, COME AND ASK ME...
AND KEEP THE SHIP RUNNING SMOOTHLY!
PULP

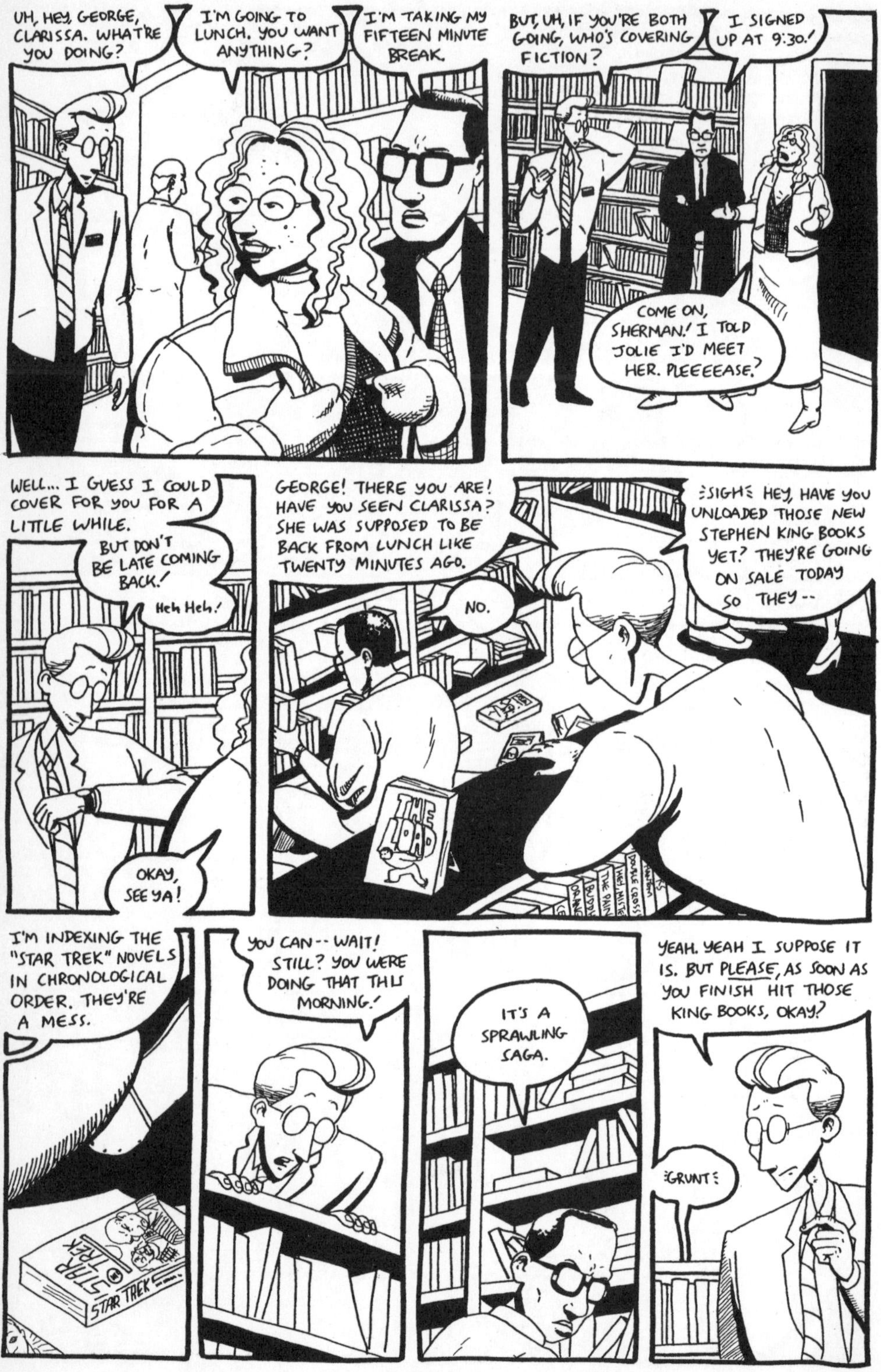
UH, HEY, GEORGE, CLARISSA. WHAT'RE YOU DOING?
I'M GOING TO LUNCH. YOU WANT ANYTHING?
I'M TAKING MY FIFTEEN MINUTE BREAK.
BUT, UH, IF YOU'RE BOTH GOING, WHO'S COVERING FICTION?
I SIGNED UP AT 9:30!
COME ON, SHERMAN! I TOLD JOLIE I'D MEET HER. PLEEEEASE?
WELL... I GUESS I COULD COVER FOR YOU FOR A LITTLE WHILE.
BUT DON'T BE LATE COMING BACK!
Heh Heh!
OKAY, SEE YA!
GEORGE! THERE YOU ARE! HAVE YOU SEEN CLARISSA? SHE WAS SUPPOSED TO BE BACK FROM LUNCH LIKE TWENTY MINUTES AGO.
NO.
:SIGH: HEY, HAVE YOU UNLOADED THOSE NEW STEPHEN KING BOOKS YET? THEY'RE GOING ON SALE TODAY SO THEY --
THE LOAD
I'M INDEXING THE "STAR TREK" NOVELS IN CHRONOLOGICAL ORDER. THEY'RE A MESS.
STAR TREK
YOU CAN-- WAIT! STILL? YOU WERE DOING THAT THIS MORNING!
IT'S A SPRAWLING SAGA.
YEAH. YEAH I SUPPOSE IT IS. BUT PLEASE, AS SOON AS YOU FINISH HIT THOSE KING BOOKS, OKAY?
:GRUNT:

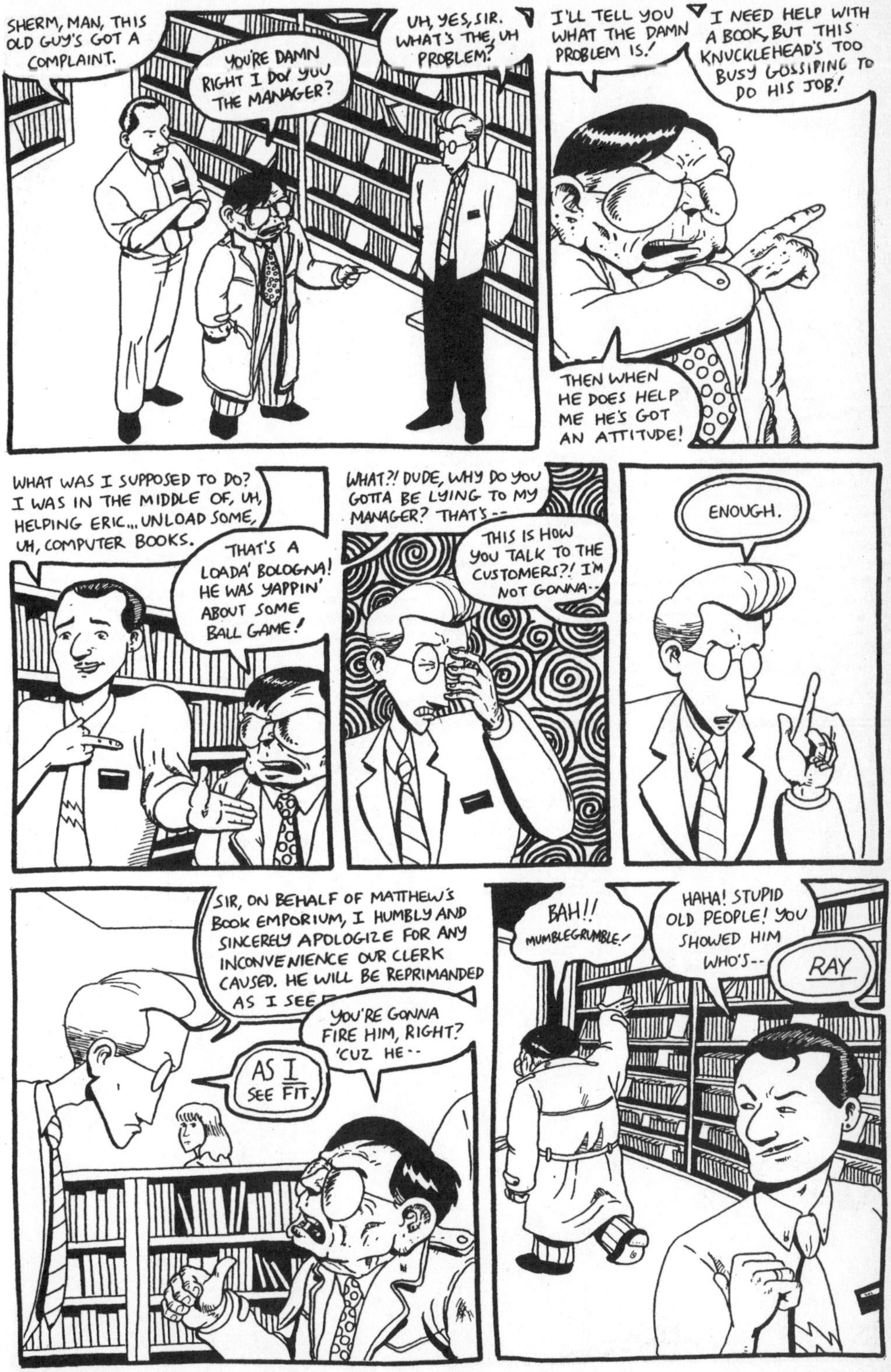
SHERM, MAN, THIS OLD GUY'S GOT A COMPLAINT.
YOU'RE DAMN RIGHT I DO! YOU THE MANAGER?
UH, YES, SIR. WHAT'S THE, UH PROBLEM?
I'LL TELL YOU WHAT THE DAMN PROBLEM IS!
I NEED HELP WITH A BOOK, BUT THIS KNUCKLEHEAD'S TOO BUSY GOSSIPING TO DO HIS JOB!
THEN WHEN HE DOES HELP ME HE'S GOT AN ATTITUDE!
WHAT WAS I SUPPOSED TO DO? I WAS IN THE MIDDLE OF, UH, HELPING ERIC... UNLOAD SOME, UH, COMPUTER BOOKS.
THAT'S A LOADA' BOLOGNA! HE WAS YAPPIN' ABOUT SOME BALL GAME!
WHAT?! DUDE, WHY DO YOU GOTTA BE LYING TO MY MANAGER? THAT'S --
THIS IS HOW YOU TALK TO THE CUSTOMERS?! I'M NOT GONNA--
ENOUGH.
SIR, ON BEHALF OF MATTHEW'S BOOK EMPORIUM, I HUMBLY AND SINCERELY APOLOGIZE FOR ANY INCONVENIENCE OUR CLERK CAUSED. HE WILL BE REPRIMANDED AS I SEE
YOU'RE GONNA FIRE HIM, RIGHT? 'CUZ HE--
AS I SEE FIT.
BAH!! MUMBLEGRUMBLE!
HAHA! STUPID OLD PEOPLE! YOU SHOWED HIM WHO'S--
RAY

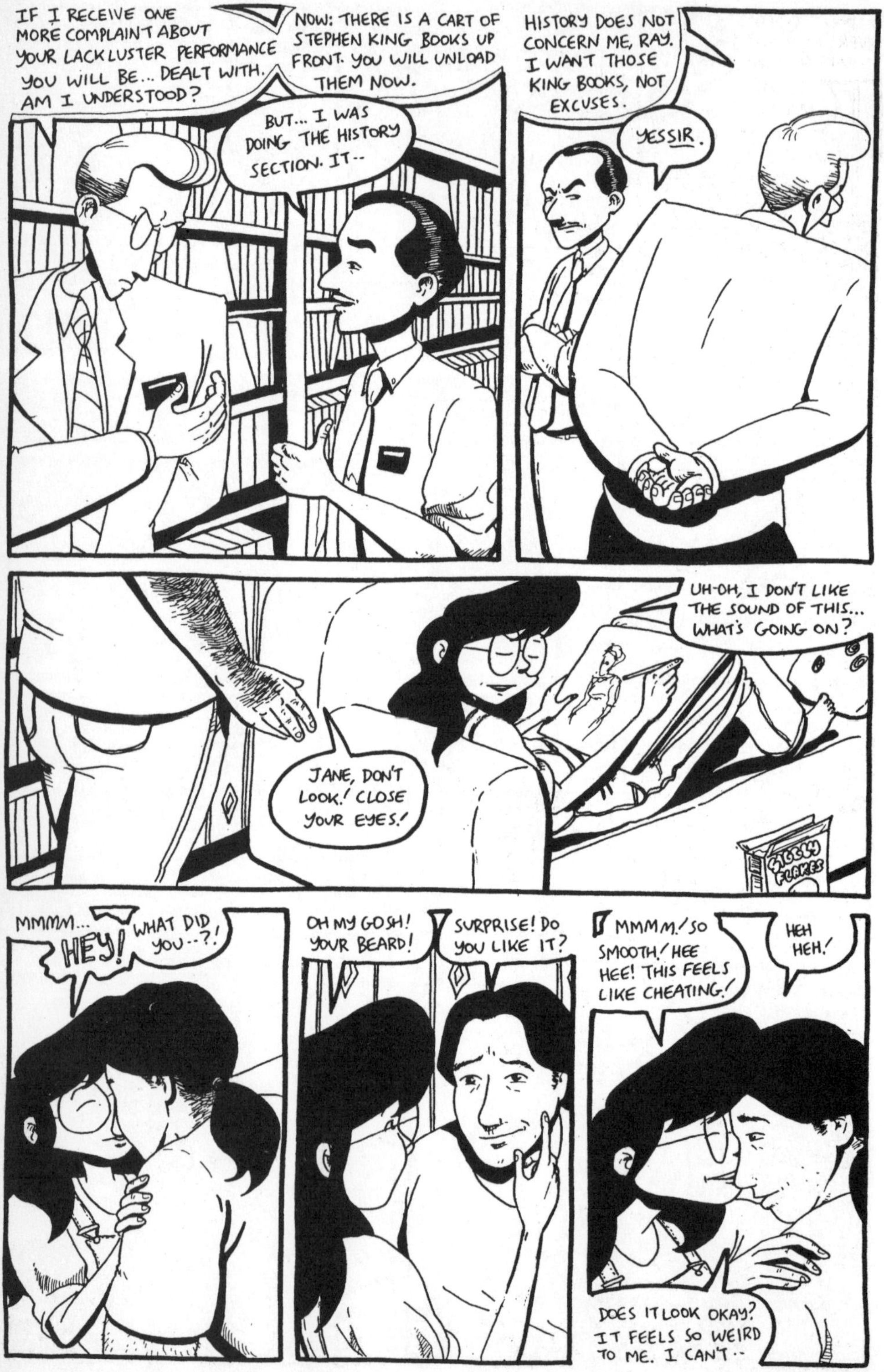
IF I RECEIVE ONE MORE COMPLAINT ABOUT YOUR LACKLUSTER PERFORMANCE YOU WILL BE... DEALT WITH. AM I UNDERSTOOD?
NOW: THERE IS A CART OF STEPHEN KING BOOKS UP FRONT. YOU WILL UNLOAD THEM NOW.
BUT... I WAS DOING THE HISTORY SECTION. IT--
HISTORY DOES NOT CONCERN ME, RAY. I WANT THOSE KING BOOKS, NOT EXCUSES.
YESSIR.
UH-OH, I DON'T LIKE THE SOUND OF THIS... WHAT'S GOING ON?
JANE, DON'T LOOK! CLOSE YOUR EYES!
MMMM...
HEY!
WHAT DID YOU--?!
OH MY GOSH! YOUR BEARD!
SURPRISE! DO YOU LIKE IT?
MMMM! SO SMOOTH! HEE HEE! THIS FEELS LIKE CHEATING!
HEH HEH!
DOES IT LOOK OKAY? IT FEELS SO WEIRD TO ME. I CAN'T--

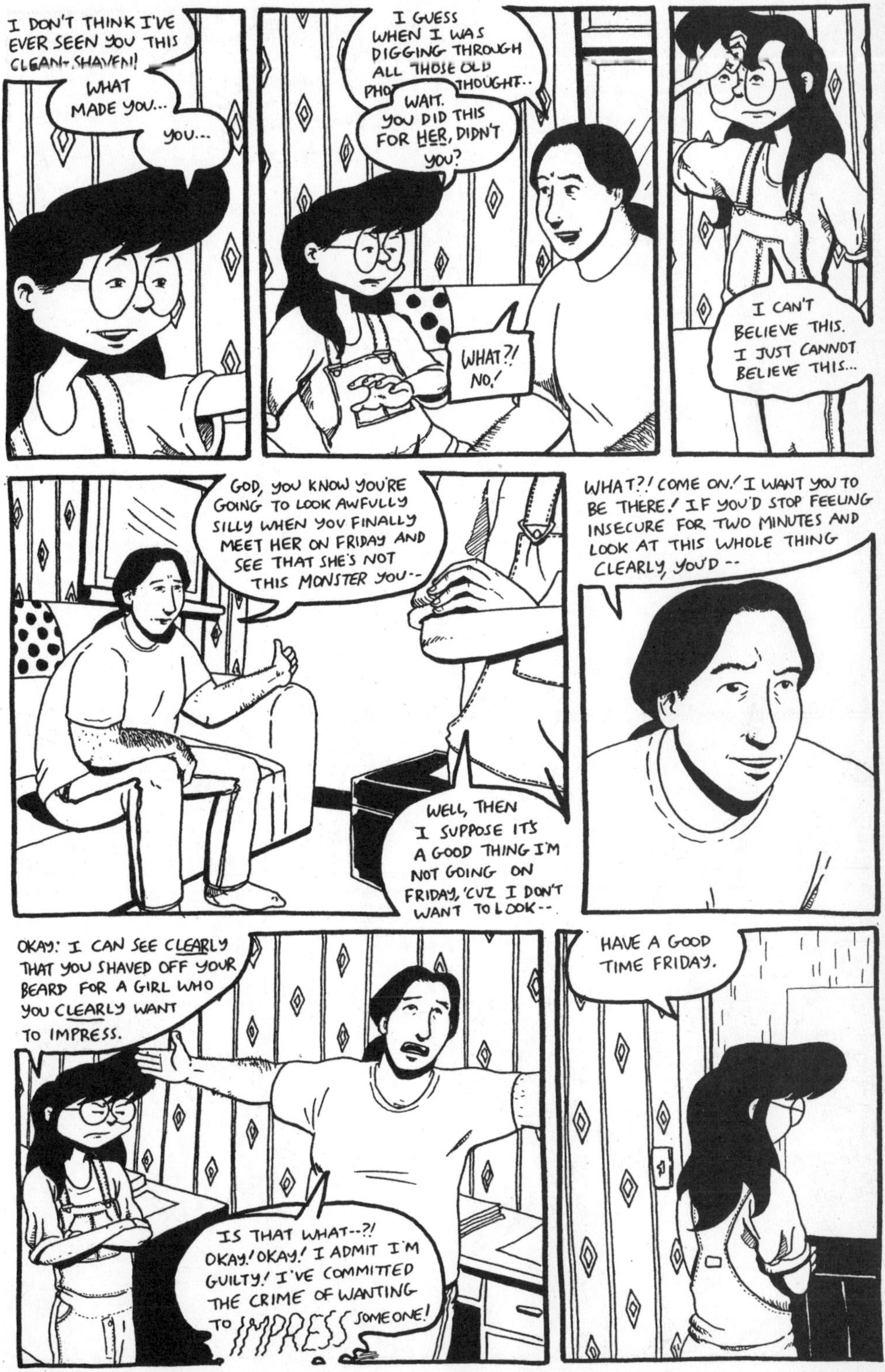
I DON'T THINK I'VE EVER SEEN YOU THIS CLEAN-SHAVEN!
WHAT MADE YOU...
YOU...
I GUESS WHEN I WAS DIGGING THROUGH ALL THOSE OLD PHO[TOS I] THOUGHT..
WAIT. YOU DID THIS FOR HER, DIDN'T YOU?
WHAT?! NO!
I CAN'T BELIEVE THIS. I JUST CANNOT BELIEVE THIS...
GOD, YOU KNOW YOU'RE GOING TO LOOK AWFULLY SILLY WHEN YOU FINALLY MEET HER ON FRIDAY AND SEE THAT SHE'S NOT THIS MONSTER YOU--
WELL, THEN I SUPPOSE IT'S A GOOD THING I'M NOT GOING ON FRIDAY, 'CUZ I DON'T WANT TO LOOK--
WHAT?! COME ON! I WANT YOU TO BE THERE! IF YOU'D STOP FEELING INSECURE FOR TWO MINUTES AND LOOK AT THIS WHOLE THING CLEARLY, YOU'D --
OKAY: I CAN SEE CLEARLY THAT YOU SHAVED OFF YOUR BEARD FOR A GIRL WHO YOU CLEARLY WANT TO IMPRESS.
IS THAT WHAT--?! OKAY! OKAY! I ADMIT I'M GUILTY! I'VE COMMITTED THE CRIME OF WANTING TO IMPRESS SOMEONE!
HAVE A GOOD TIME FRIDAY.

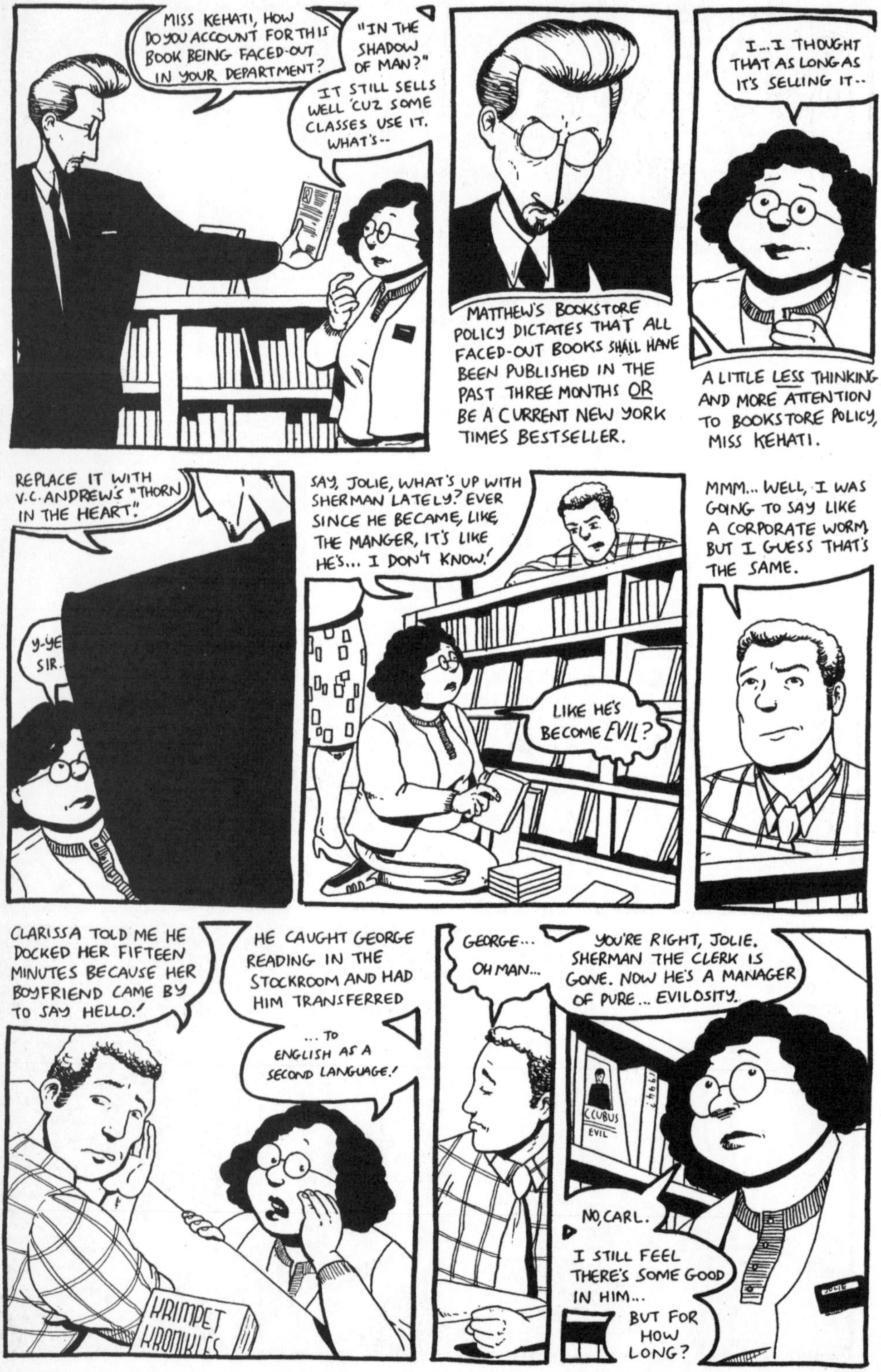
MISS KEHATI, HOW DO YOU ACCOUNT FOR THIS BOOK BEING FACED-OUT IN YOUR DEPARTMENT?
"IN THE SHADOW OF MAN?"
IT STILL SELLS WELL 'CUZ SOME CLASSES USE IT. WHAT'S--
MATTHEW'S BOOKSTORE POLICY DICTATES THAT ALL FACED-OUT BOOKS SHALL HAVE BEEN PUBLISHED IN THE PAST THREE MONTHS OR BE A CURRENT NEW YORK TIMES BESTSELLER.
I...I THOUGHT THAT AS LONG AS IT'S SELLING IT--
A LITTLE LESS THINKING AND MORE ATTENTION TO BOOKSTORE POLICY, MISS KEHATI.
REPLACE IT WITH V.C. ANDREW'S "THORN IN THE HEART."
Y-YES SIR.
SAY, JOLIE, WHAT'S UP WITH SHERMAN LATELY? EVER SINCE HE BECAME, LIKE, THE MANGER, IT'S LIKE HE'S... I DON'T KNOW!
LIKE HE'S BECOME EVIL?
MMM... WELL, I WAS GOING TO SAY LIKE A CORPORATE WORM BUT I GUESS THAT'S THE SAME.
CLARISSA TOLD ME HE DOCKED HER FIFTEEN MINUTES BECAUSE HER BOYFRIEND CAME BY TO SAY HELLO!
HE CAUGHT GEORGE READING IN THE STOCKROOM AND HAD HIM TRANSFERRED
... TO ENGLISH AS A SECOND LANGUAGE!
KRIMPET KRONIKLES
GEORGE...
OH MAN...
YOU'RE RIGHT, JOLIE. SHERMAN THE CLERK IS GONE. NOW HE'S A MANAGER OF PURE... EVILOSITY.
1994
CLUBUS
EVIL
NO, CARL.
I STILL FEEL THERE'S SOME GOOD IN HIM...
BUT FOR HOW LONG?
JULIE

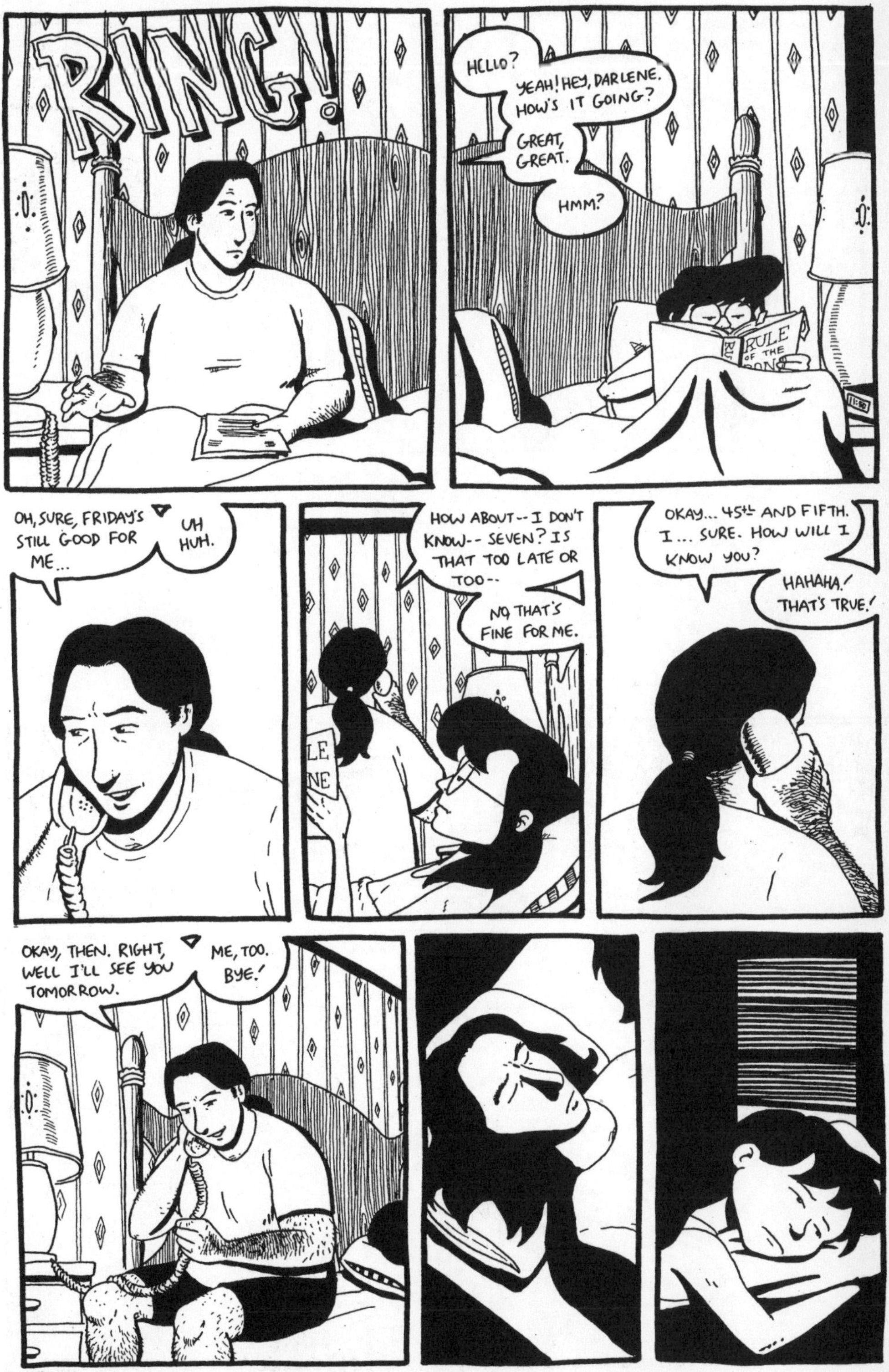

RING!
HELLO?
YEAH! HEY, DARLENE. HOW'S IT GOING?
GREAT, GREAT.
HMM?
RULE OF THE BONE
OH, SURE, FRIDAY'S STILL GOOD FOR ME...
UH HUH.
HOW ABOUT-- I DON'T KNOW-- SEVEN? IS THAT TOO LATE OR TOO--
NO, THAT'S FINE FOR ME.
OKAY... 45th AND FIFTH. I... SURE. HOW WILL I KNOW YOU?
HAHAHA! THAT'S TRUE!
OKAY, THEN. RIGHT, WELL I'LL SEE YOU TOMORROW.
ME, TOO. BYE!

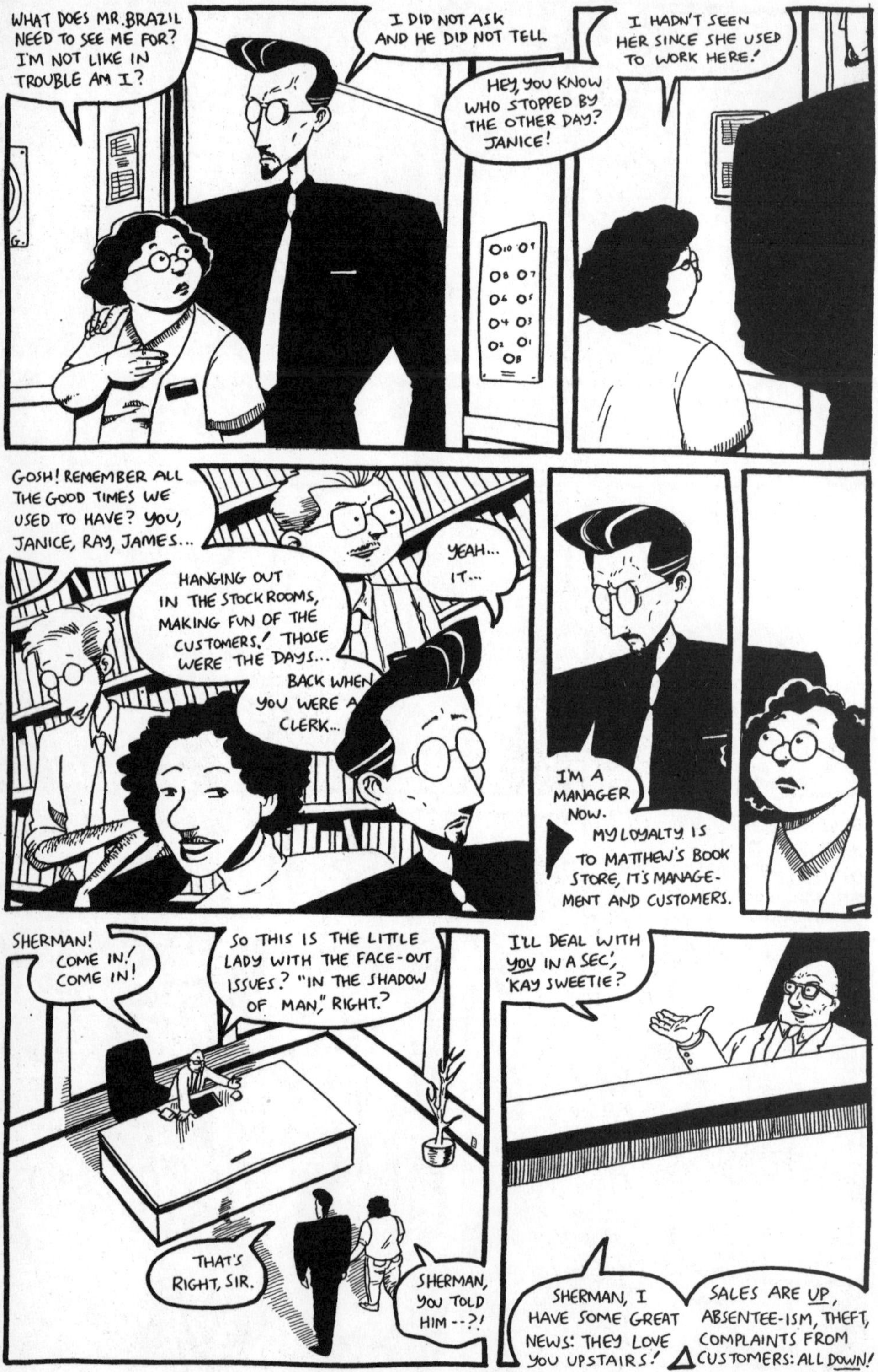
WHAT DOES MR. BRAZIL NEED TO SEE ME FOR? I'M NOT LIKE IN TROUBLE AM I?
I DID NOT ASK AND HE DID NOT TELL
HEY, YOU KNOW WHO STOPPED BY THE OTHER DAY? JANICE!
I HADN'T SEEN HER SINCE SHE USED TO WORK HERE!
GOSH! REMEMBER ALL THE GOOD TIMES WE USED TO HAVE? YOU, JANICE, RAY, JAMES...
HANGING OUT IN THE STOCK ROOMS, MAKING FUN OF THE CUSTOMERS! THOSE WERE THE DAYS...
YEAH... IT...
BACK WHEN YOU WERE A CLERK...
I'M A MANAGER NOW.
MY LOYALTY IS TO MATTHEW'S BOOK STORE, IT'S MANAGEMENT AND CUSTOMERS.
SHERMAN! COME IN! COME IN!
SO THIS IS THE LITTLE LADY WITH THE FACE-OUT ISSUES? "IN THE SHADOW OF MAN," RIGHT?
THAT'S RIGHT, SIR.
SHERMAN, YOU TOLD HIM --?!
I'LL DEAL WITH YOU IN A SEC, 'KAY SWEETIE?
SHERMAN, I HAVE SOME GREAT NEWS: THEY LOVE YOU UPSTAIRS!
SALES ARE UP, ABSENTEE-ISM, THEFT, COMPLAINTS FROM CUSTOMERS: ALL DOWN!

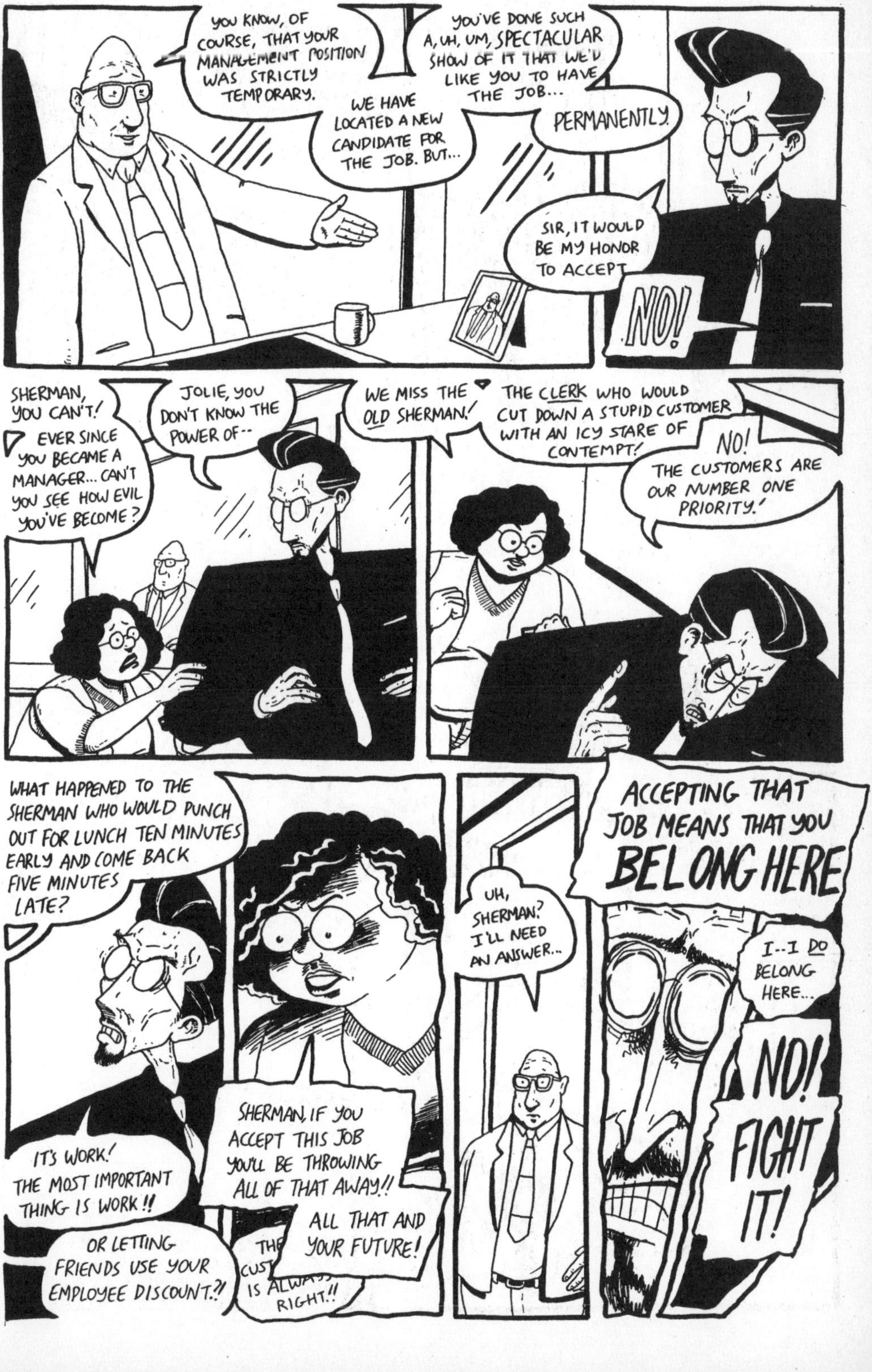
YOU KNOW, OF COURSE, THAT YOUR MANAGEMENT POSITION WAS STRICTLY TEMPORARY.
WE HAVE LOCATED A NEW CANDIDATE FOR THE JOB. BUT...
YOU'VE DONE SUCH A, UH, UM, SPECTACULAR SHOW OF IT THAT WE'D LIKE YOU TO HAVE THE JOB...
PERMANENTLY.
SIR, IT WOULD BE MY HONOR TO ACCEPT
NO!
SHERMAN, YOU CAN'T!
EVER SINCE YOU BECAME A MANAGER... CAN'T YOU SEE HOW EVIL YOU'VE BECOME?
JOLIE, YOU DON'T KNOW THE POWER OF--
WE MISS THE OLD SHERMAN!
THE CLERK WHO WOULD CUT DOWN A STUPID CUSTOMER WITH AN ICY STARE OF CONTEMPT!
NO! THE CUSTOMERS ARE OUR NUMBER ONE PRIORITY!
WHAT HAPPENED TO THE SHERMAN WHO WOULD PUNCH OUT FOR LUNCH TEN MINUTES EARLY AND COME BACK FIVE MINUTES LATE?
IT'S WORK! THE MOST IMPORTANT THING IS WORK!!
OR LETTING FRIENDS USE YOUR EMPLOYEE DISCOUNT?!
SHERMAN, IF YOU ACCEPT THIS JOB YOU'LL BE THROWING ALL OF THAT AWAY!!
ALL THAT AND YOUR FUTURE!
RIGHT!!
UH, SHERMAN? I'LL NEED AN ANSWER...
ACCEPTING THAT JOB MEANS THAT YOU BELONG HERE
I--I DO BELONG HERE...
NO! FIGHT IT!

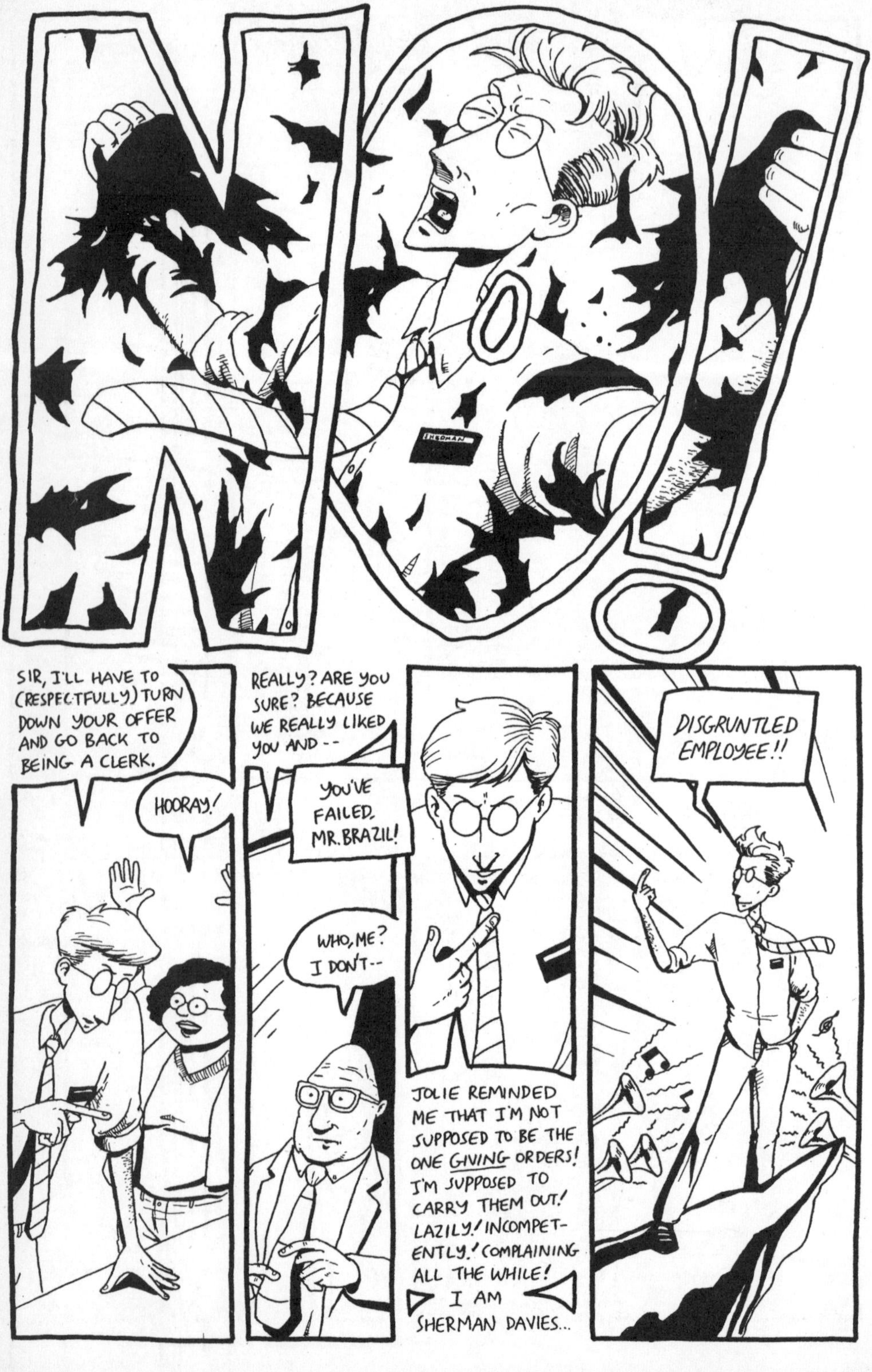
NO!
SHERMAN
SIR, I'LL HAVE TO (RESPECTFULLY) TURN DOWN YOUR OFFER AND GO BACK TO BEING A CLERK.
HOORAY!
REALLY? ARE YOU SURE? BECAUSE WE REALLY LIKED YOU AND --
YOU'VE FAILED, MR. BRAZIL!
WHO, ME? I DON'T--
JOLIE REMINDED ME THAT I'M NOT SUPPOSED TO BE THE ONE GIVING ORDERS! I'M SUPPOSED TO CARRY THEM OUT! LAZILY! INCOMPETENTLY! COMPLAINING ALL THE WHILE!
I AM SHERMAN DAVIES...
DISGRUNTLED EMPLOYEE!!

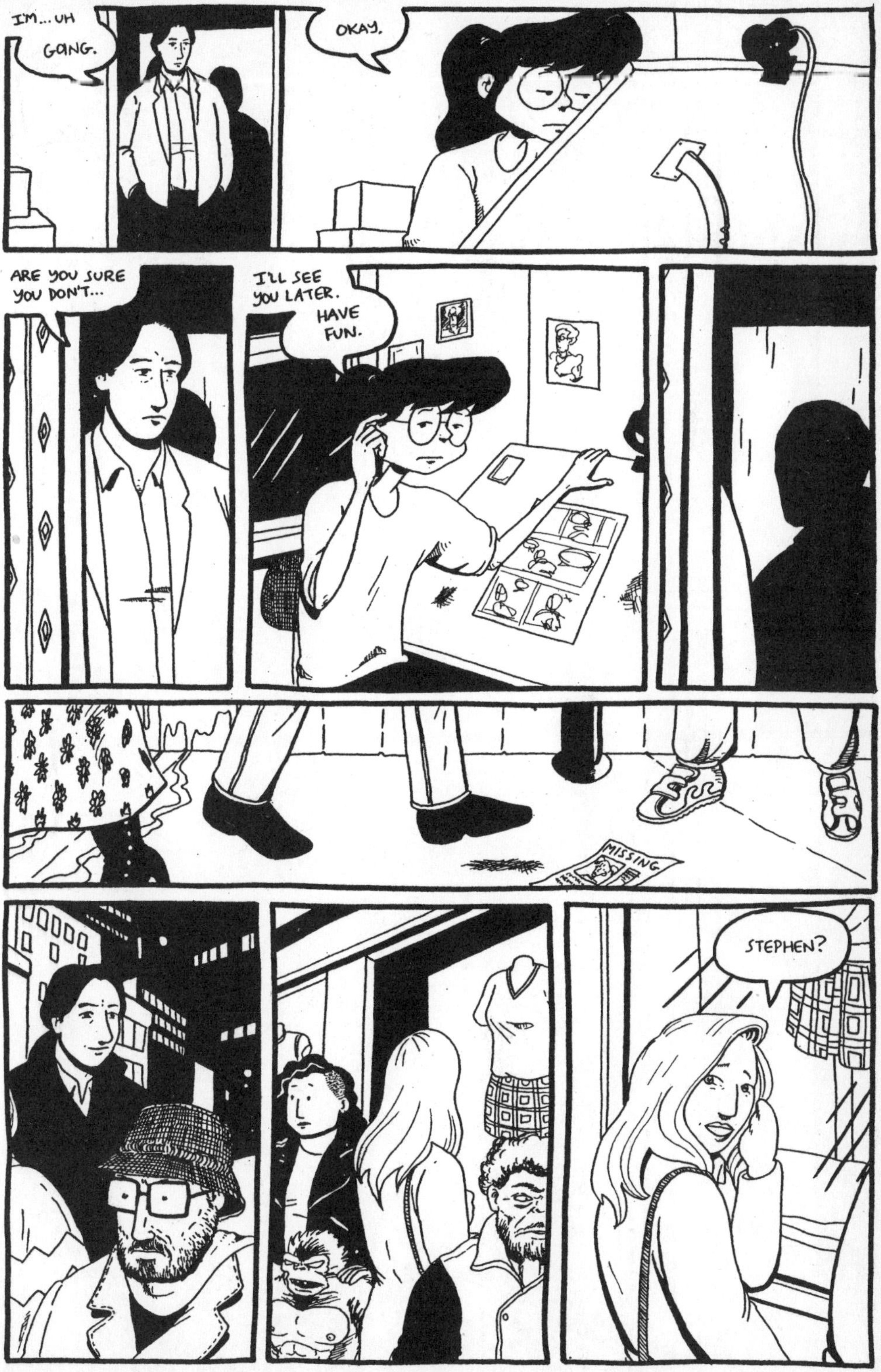
I'M... UH GOING.
OKAY.
ARE YOU SURE YOU DON'T...
I'LL SEE YOU LATER.
HAVE FUN.
MISSING
STEPHEN?

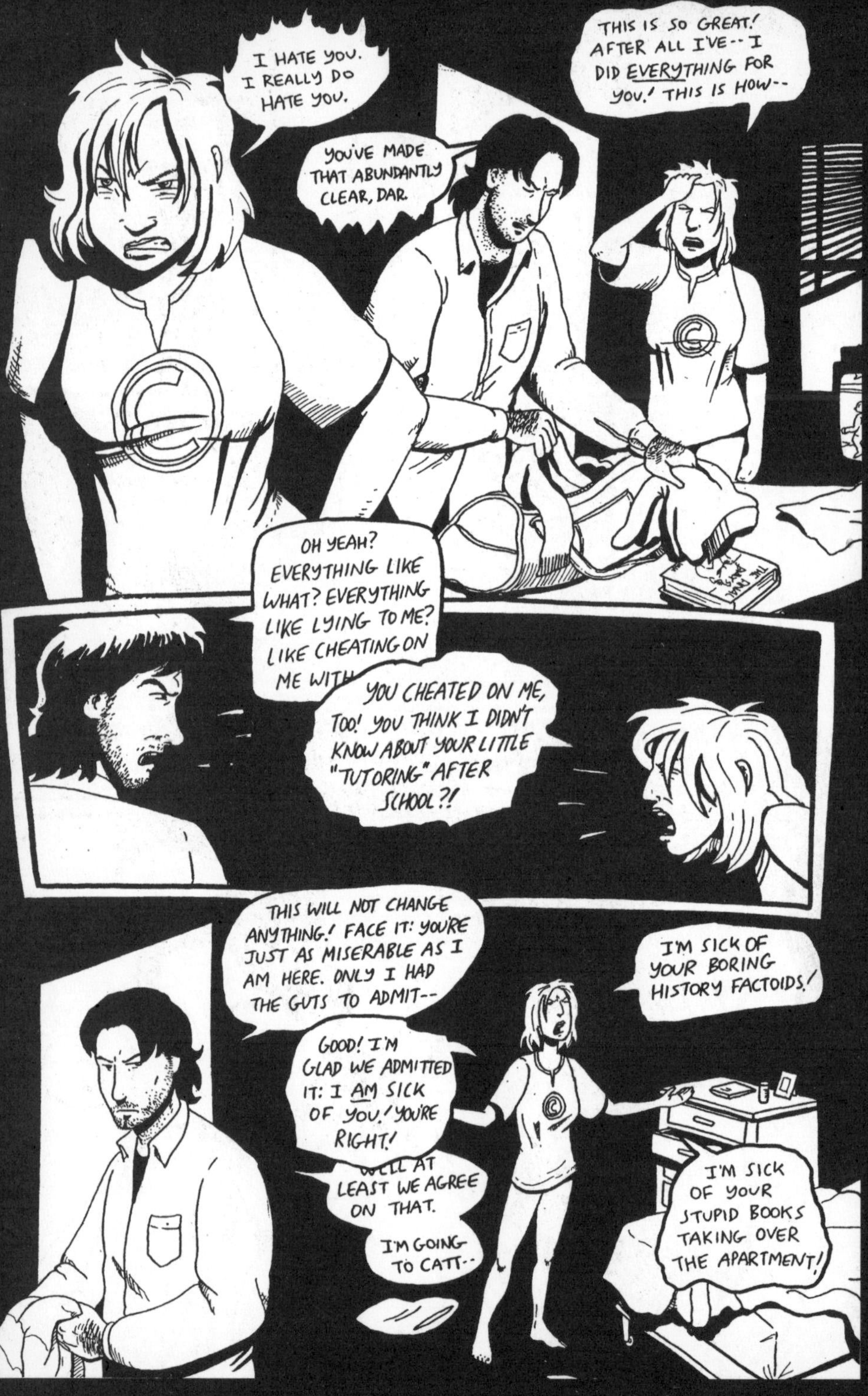
I HATE YOU. I REALLY DO HATE YOU.
YOU'VE MADE THAT ABUNDANTLY CLEAR, DAR.
THIS IS SO GREAT! AFTER ALL I'VE-- I DID EVERYTHING FOR YOU! THIS IS HOW--
OH YEAH? EVERYTHING LIKE WHAT? EVERYTHING LIKE LYING TO ME? LIKE CHEATING ON ME WITH
YOU CHEATED ON ME, TOO! YOU THINK I DIDN'T KNOW ABOUT YOUR LITTLE "TUTORING" AFTER SCHOOL?!
THIS WILL NOT CHANGE ANYTHING! FACE IT: YOU'RE JUST AS MISERABLE AS I AM HERE. ONLY I HAD THE GUTS TO ADMIT--
I'M SICK OF YOUR BORING HISTORY FACTOIDS!
GOOD! I'M GLAD WE ADMITTED IT: I AM SICK OF YOU! YOU'RE RIGHT!
WELL AT LEAST WE AGREE ON THAT.
I'M GOING TO CATT--
I'M SICK OF YOUR STUPID BOOKS TAKING OVER THE APARTMENT!

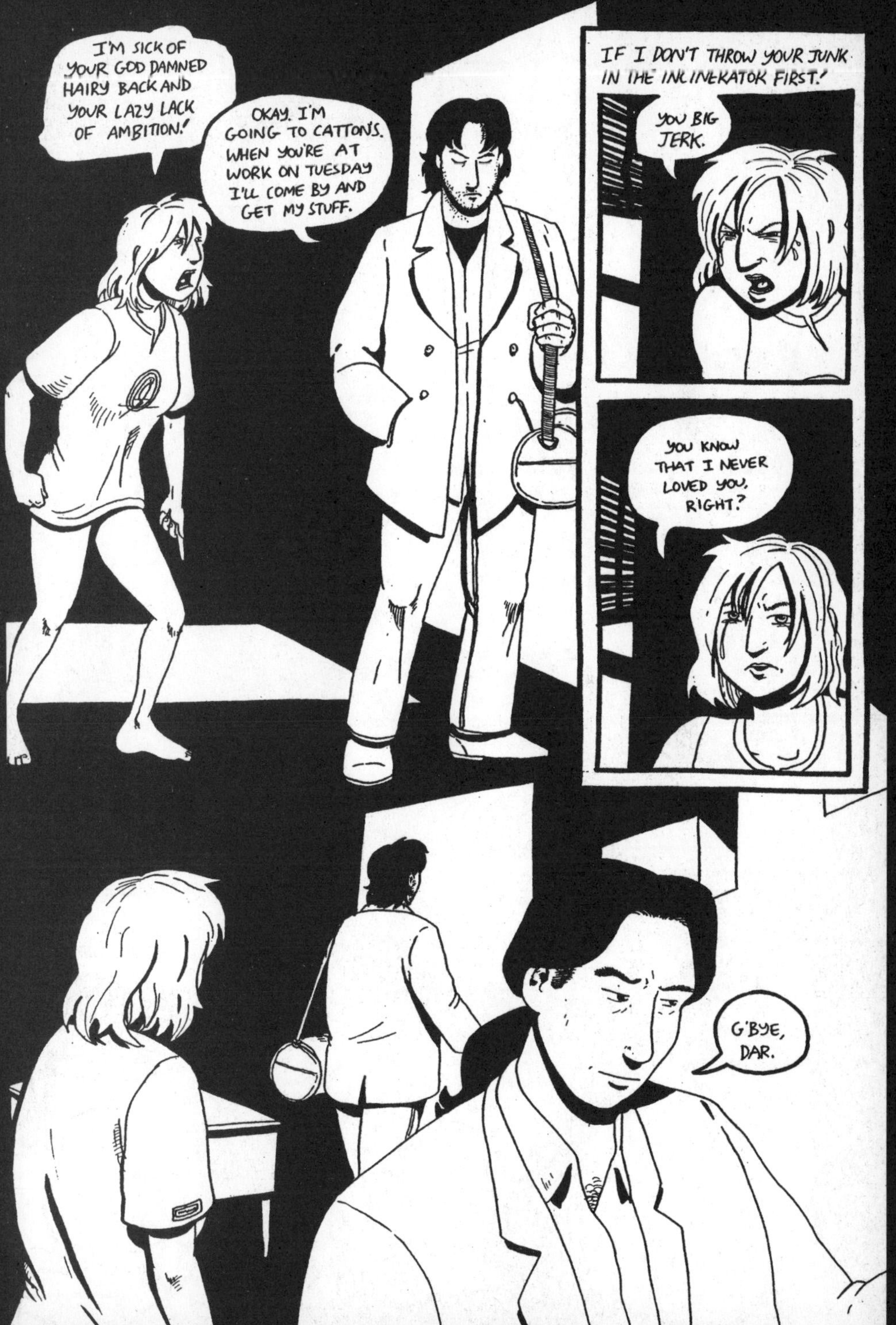
I'M SICK OF YOUR GOD DAMNED HAIRY BACK AND YOUR LAZY LACK OF AMBITION!
OKAY. I'M GOING TO CATTON'S. WHEN YOU'RE AT WORK ON TUESDAY I'LL COME BY AND GET MY STUFF.
IF I DON'T THROW YOUR JUNK IN THE INCINERATOR FIRST!
YOU BIG JERK.
YOU KNOW THAT I NEVER LOVED YOU, RIGHT?
G'BYE, DAR.

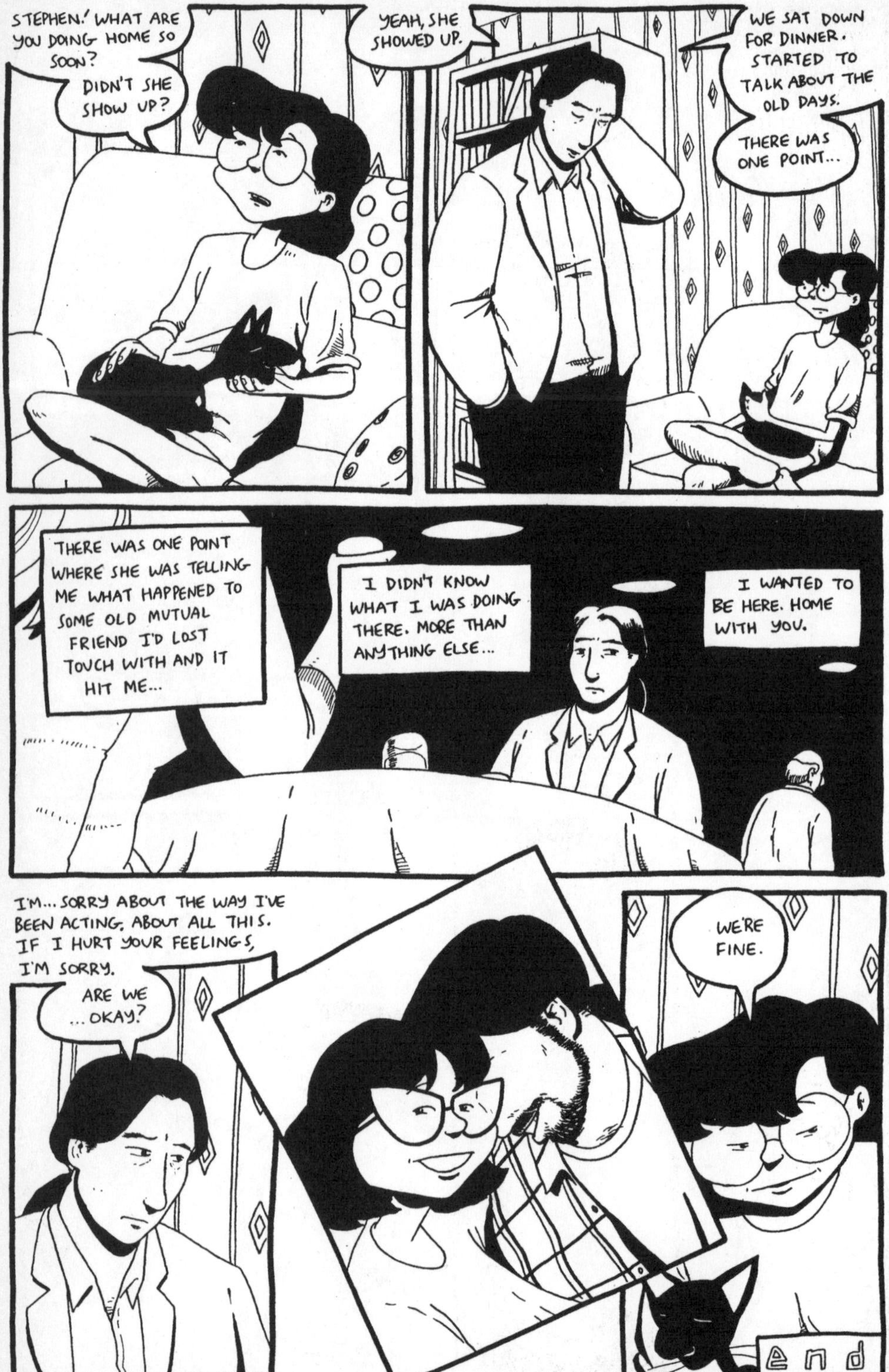

STEPHEN! WHAT ARE YOU DOING HOME SO SOON?
DIDN'T SHE SHOW UP?
YEAH, SHE SHOWED UP.
WE SAT DOWN FOR DINNER. STARTED TO TALK ABOUT THE OLD DAYS.
THERE WAS ONE POINT...
THERE WAS ONE POINT WHERE SHE WAS TELLING ME WHAT HAPPENED TO SOME OLD MUTUAL FRIEND I'D LOST TOUCH WITH AND IT HIT ME...
I DIDN'T KNOW WHAT I WAS DOING THERE. MORE THAN ANYTHING ELSE...
I WANTED TO BE HERE. HOME WITH YOU.
I'M... SORRY ABOUT THE WAY I'VE BEEN ACTING, ABOUT ALL THIS. IF I HURT YOUR FEELINGS, I'M SORRY.
ARE WE ...OKAY?
WE'RE FINE.
end

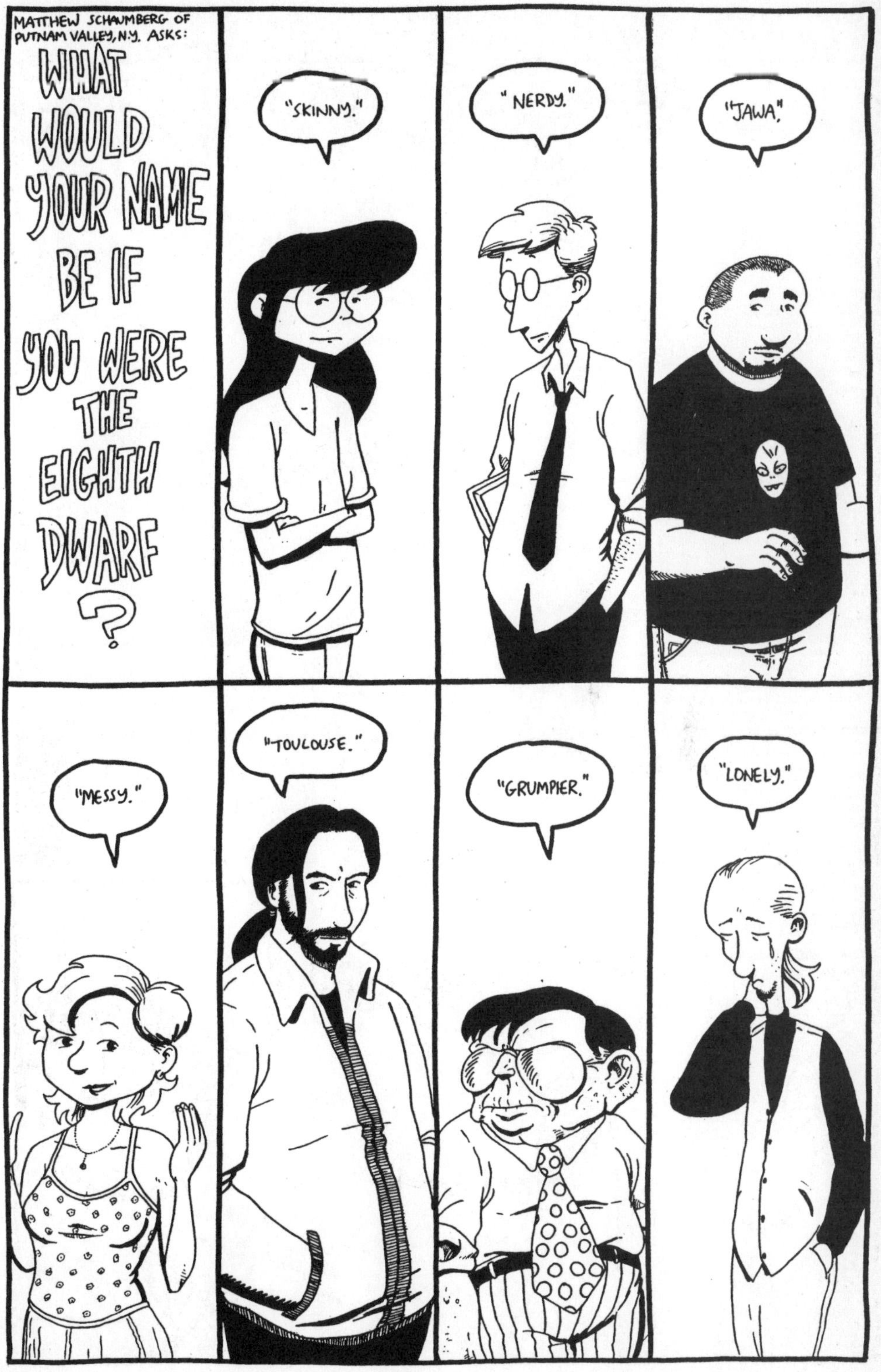
MATTHEW SCHAUMBERG OF PUTNAM VALLEY, N.Y. ASKS:
WHAT WOULD YOUR NAME BE IF YOU WERE THE EIGHTH DWARF ?
"SKINNY."
"NERDY."
"JAWA."
"MESSY."
"TOULOUSE."
"GRUMPIER."
"LONELY."

JANE'S HIGH SCHOOL REUNION by ALEX ROBINSON

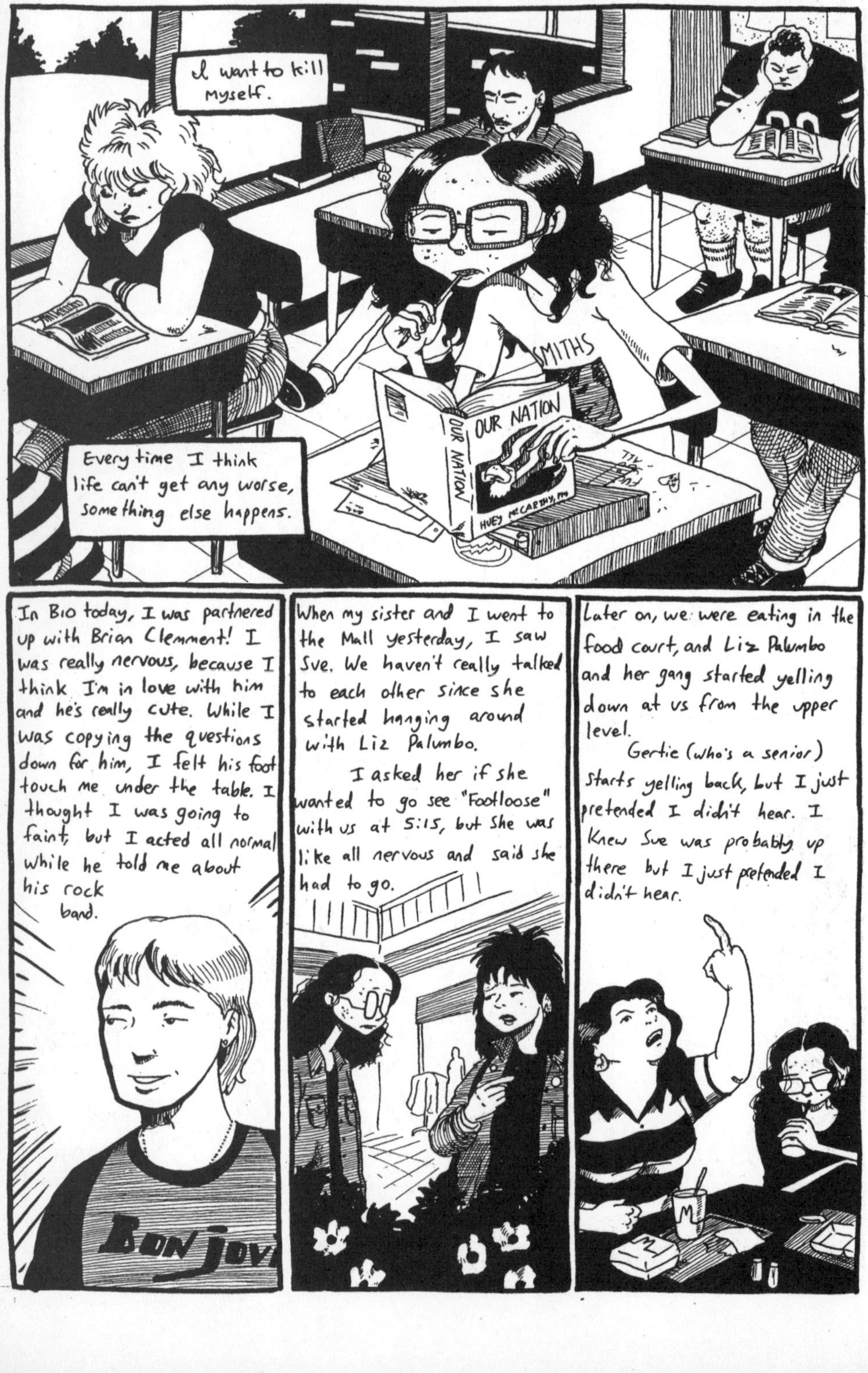
I want to kill myself.
SMITHS
OUR NATION
OUR NATION
Every time I think life can't get any worse, something else happens.
In Bio today, I was partnered up with Brian Clemment! I was really nervous, because I think I'm in love with him and he's really cute. While I was copying the questions down for him, I felt his foot touch me under the table. I thought I was going to faint, but I acted all normal while he told me about his rock band.
BON JOVI
When my sister and I went to the Mall yesterday, I saw Sue. We haven't really talked to each other since she started hanging around with Liz Palumbo.
I asked her if she wanted to go see "Footloose" with us at 5:15, but she was like all nervous and said she had to go.
Later on, we were eating in the food court, and Liz Palumbo and her gang started yelling down at us from the upper level.
Gertie (who's a senior) starts yelling back, but I just pretended I didn't hear. I knew Sue was probably up there but I just pretended I didn't hear.
M

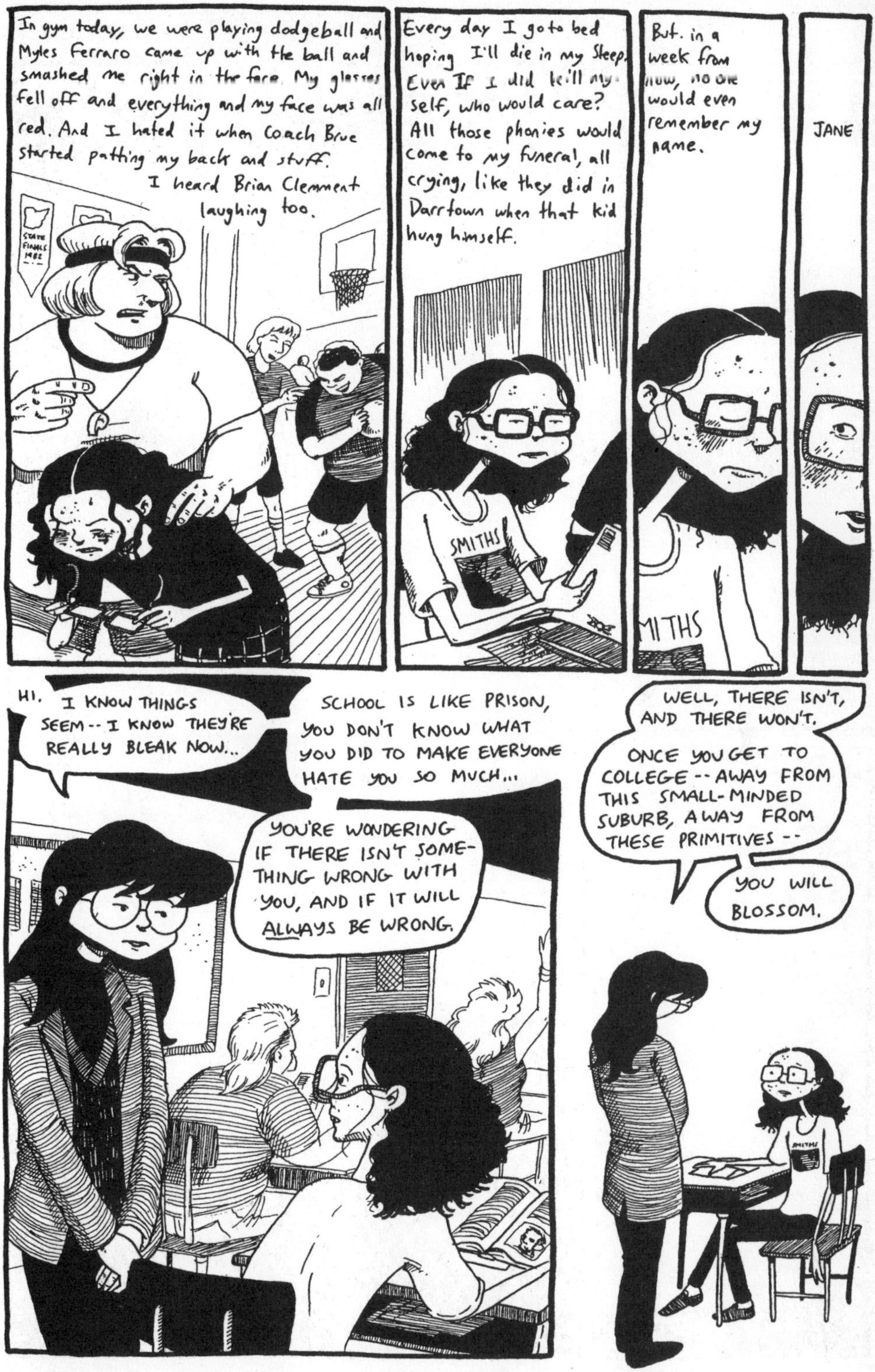
In gym today, we were playing dodgeball and Myles Ferraro came up with the ball and smashed me right in the face. My glasses fell off and everything and my face was all red. And I hated it when Coach Brue started patting my back and stuff.
I heard Brian Clemment laughing too.
STATE FINALS 1982
Every day I go to bed hoping I'll die in my sleep. Even If I did kill my-self, who would care? All those phonies would come to my funeral, all crying, like they did in Darrtown when that kid hung himself.
SMITHS
But. in a week from now, no one would even remember my name.
SMITHS
JANE
HI. I KNOW THINGS SEEM -- I KNOW THEY'RE REALLY BLEAK NOW...
SCHOOL IS LIKE PRISON, YOU DON'T KNOW WHAT YOU DID TO MAKE EVERYONE HATE YOU SO MUCH...
YOU'RE WONDERING IF THERE ISN'T SOME-THING WRONG WITH YOU, AND IF IT WILL ALWAYS BE WRONG.
WELL, THERE ISN'T, AND THERE WON'T.
ONCE YOU GET TO COLLEGE -- AWAY FROM THIS SMALL-MINDED SUBURB, AWAY FROM THESE PRIMITIVES --
YOU WILL BLOSSOM.
SMITHS

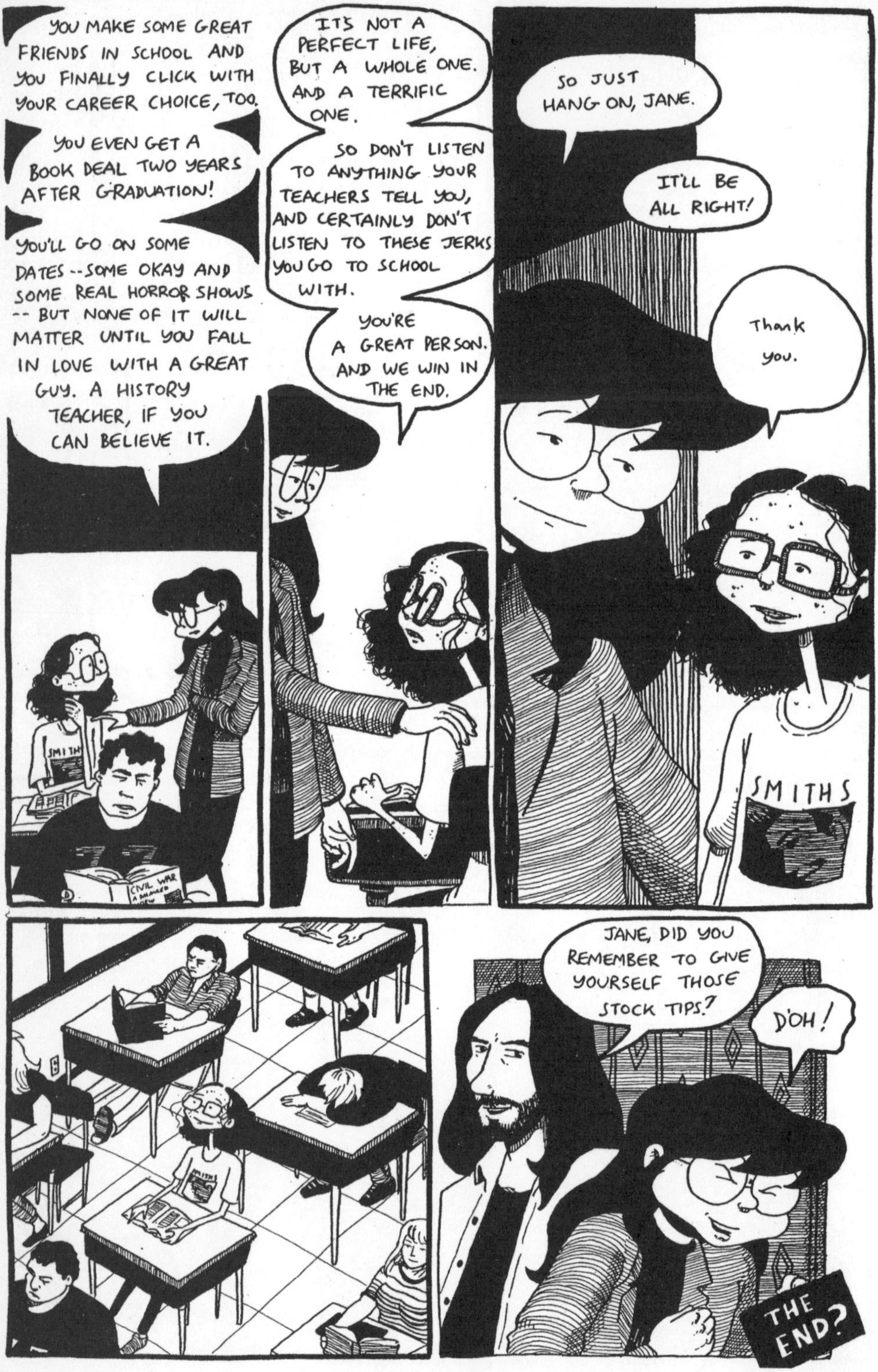
YOU MAKE SOME GREAT FRIENDS IN SCHOOL AND YOU FINALLY CLICK WITH YOUR CAREER CHOICE, TOO.
YOU EVEN GET A BOOK DEAL TWO YEARS AFTER GRADUATION!
YOU'LL GO ON SOME DATES -- SOME OKAY AND SOME REAL HORROR SHOWS -- BUT NONE OF IT WILL MATTER UNTIL YOU FALL IN LOVE WITH A GREAT GUY. A HISTORY TEACHER, IF YOU CAN BELIEVE IT.
SMITHS
CIVIL WAR
IT'S NOT A PERFECT LIFE, BUT A WHOLE ONE. AND A TERRIFIC ONE.
SO DON'T LISTEN TO ANYTHING YOUR TEACHERS TELL YOU, AND CERTAINLY DON'T LISTEN TO THESE JERKS YOU GO TO SCHOOL WITH.
YOU'RE A GREAT PERSON. AND WE WIN IN THE END.
SO JUST HANG ON, JANE.
IT'LL BE ALL RIGHT!
Thank you.
SMITHS
JANE, DID YOU REMEMBER TO GIVE YOURSELF THOSE STOCK TIPS?
D'OH!
THE END?

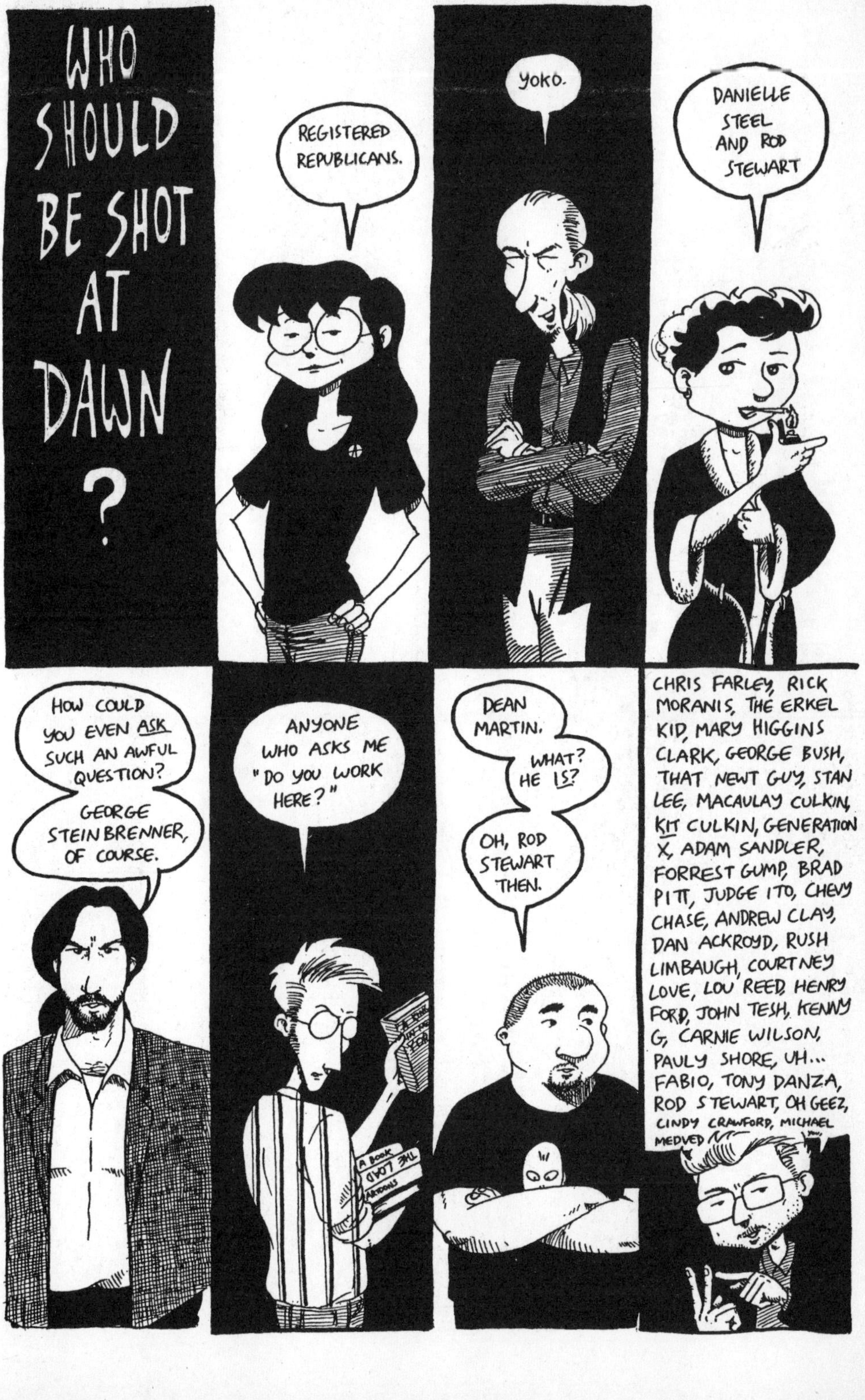
WHO SHOULD BE SHOT AT DAWN ?
REGISTERED REPUBLICANS.
YOKO.
DANIELLE STEEL AND ROD STEWART
HOW COULD YOU EVEN ASK SUCH AN AWFUL QUESTION?
GEORGE STEINBRENNER, OF COURSE.
ANYONE WHO ASKS ME "DO YOU WORK HERE?"
DEAN MARTIN.
WHAT? HE IS?
OH, ROD STEWART THEN.
CHRIS FARLEY, RICK MORANIS, THE ERKEL KID, MARY HIGGINS CLARK, GEORGE BUSH, THAT NEWT GUY, STAN LEE, MACAULAY CULKIN, KIT CULKIN, GENERATION X, ADAM SANDLER, FORREST GUMP, BRAD PITT, JUDGE ITO, CHEVY CHASE, ANDREW CLAY, DAN ACKROYD, RUSH LIMBAUGH, COURTNEY LOVE, LOU REED, HENRY FORD, JOHN TESH, KENNY G, CARNIE WILSON, PAULY SHORE, UH... FABIO, TONY DANZA, ROD STEWART, OH GEEZ, CINDY CRAWFORD, MICHAEL MEDVED

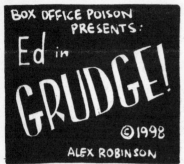

BOX OFFICE POISON PRESENTS:

Ed in GRUDGE!

©1998

ALEX ROBINSON

YEAH, WELL MY ASS IS GETTIN' IN FOR FREE, WHILE YOUR COSTUMELESS ASS IS PAYIN' $2.50!

THAT'S $2.50 WORTH OF COMICS I'LL HAVE THAT YOUR SORRY ASS WON'T!

WHO CARES? THE ONLY REASON I CAME IS TO SHOW MY DRAWINGS TO DAVE NORG-STROMME!

I CAN'T BELIEVE YOU REALLY WORE THAT DUMB THING!

THAT GUY WHO DRAWS "REVENGE CORPS?" HE WON'T GIVE YOU NO JOB, STOOPIT!

I KNOW! I JUST WANT TO SHOW HIM MY STUFF SO HE CAN TELL ME IF I'M GOOD.

HOLY CRAP!! "GOOD?!" YOU'RE FREAKIN' AY-MAZING!!

THESE PAGES ARE FANTASTIC! ARE YOU SURE YOU'RE ONLY FIFTEEN, KID?!

WELL... YOU KNOW HOW IT IS... HEH, HEH...

FINAL!

DAILY BUGLE

QUEENS BOY TO HELM X-MEN

"NO, PLEASE MR. LEE, I-- OKAY, I'LL CALL YOU STAN, BUT THIS CHECK, IT'S TOO--"

ED! C'MON, MAN! THEY'RE LETTIN' US IN!

artists alley

UH, EXCUSE ME, MISTER. DO YOU KNOW WHEN DAVE NORGSTROMME IS GONNA BE HERE?

WHO? NAH, I DON'T KNOW NOTHIN' ABOUT IT.

YOU'RE AN ARTIST? HERE, COME HERE, I'LL LOOK AT YOUR STUFF. GIVE YOU SOME POINTERS.

UH, NO THANKS. I'LL JUST WAIT.

SUIT YOURSELF

YOU LITTLE BASTARD.

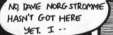

YOU READY TO GO YET, MAN? WE BEEN HERE AN' HOUR.

NO, DAVE NORGSTROMME HASN'T GOT HERE YET. I --

COME ON, HE'S NOT SHOWING UP. 'SIDES, MAN, THIS CAPE IS ITCHING MY NECK!

JUST TEN MORE MINUTES, HECTOR, IF HE --

OH MY GOD!

THERE HE IS! HE'S HERE!

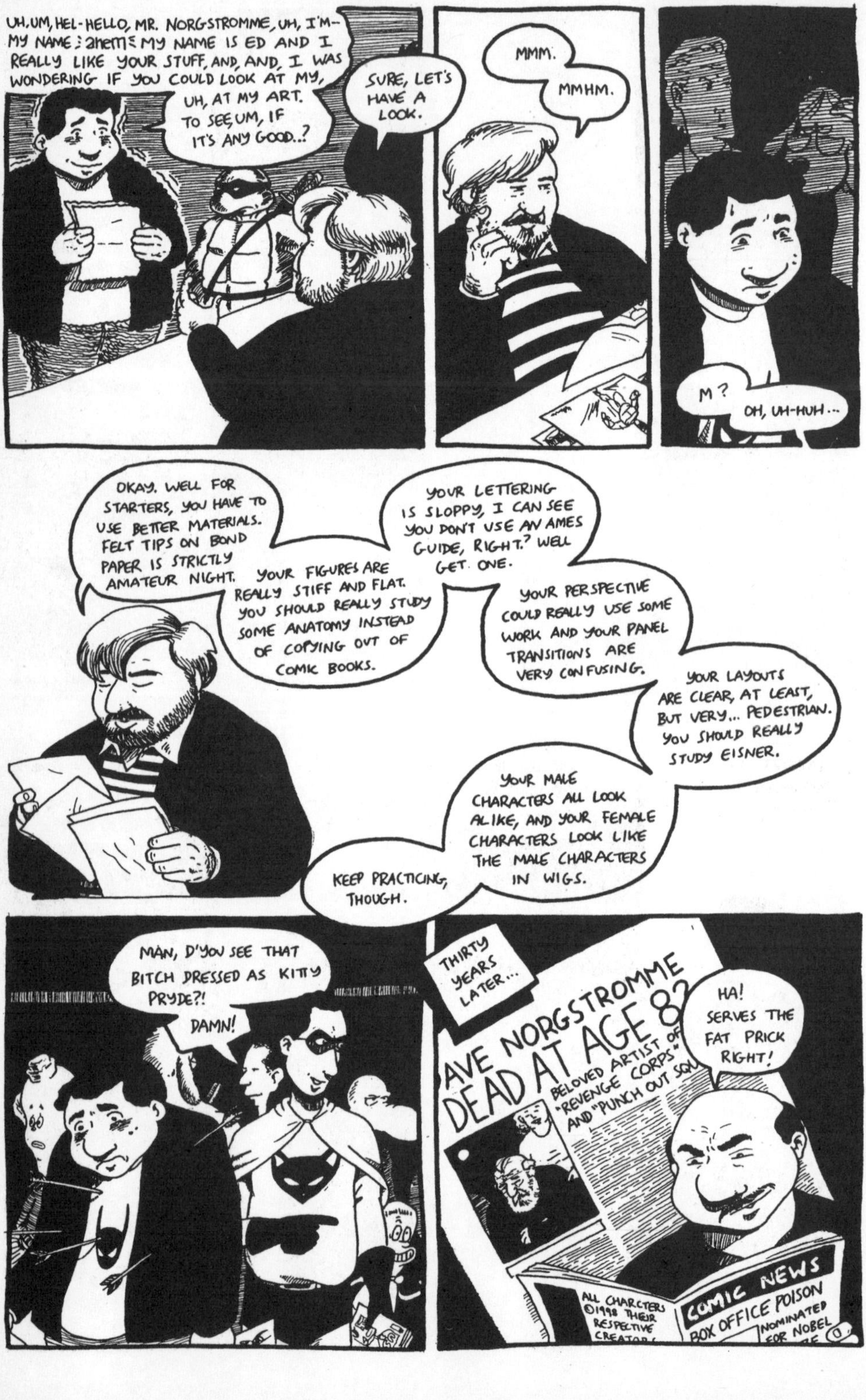
UH, UM, HEL-HELLO, MR. NORGSTROMME, UH, I'M- MY NAME :ahem: MY NAME IS ED AND I REALLY LIKE YOUR STUFF, AND, AND, I WAS WONDERING IF YOU COULD LOOK AT MY,
UH, AT MY ART. TO SEE, UM, IF IT'S ANY GOOD..?
SURE, LET'S HAVE A LOOK.
MMM.
MMHM.
M?
OH, UH-HUH...
OKAY. WELL FOR STARTERS, YOU HAVE TO USE BETTER MATERIALS. FELT TIPS ON BOND PAPER IS STRICTLY AMATEUR NIGHT.
YOUR FIGURES ARE REALLY STIFF AND FLAT. YOU SHOULD REALLY STUDY SOME ANATOMY INSTEAD OF COPYING OUT OF COMIC BOOKS.
YOUR LETTERING IS SLOPPY, I CAN SEE YOU DON'T USE AN AMES GUIDE, RIGHT? WELL GET ONE.
YOUR PERSPECTIVE COULD REALLY USE SOME WORK AND YOUR PANEL TRANSITIONS ARE VERY CONFUSING.
YOUR LAYOUTS ARE CLEAR, AT LEAST, BUT VERY... PEDESTRIAN. YOU SHOULD REALLY STUDY EISNER.
YOUR MALE CHARACTERS ALL LOOK ALIKE, AND YOUR FEMALE CHARACTERS LOOK LIKE THE MALE CHARACTERS IN WIGS.
KEEP PRACTICING, THOUGH.
MAN, D'YOU SEE THAT BITCH DRESSED AS KITTY PRYDE?!
DAMN!
THIRTY YEARS LATER...
AVE NORGSTROMME DEAD AT AGE 82
BELOVED ARTIST OF "REVENGE CORPS" AND "PUNCH OUT SQU
HA! SERVES THE FAT PRICK RIGHT!
COMIC NEWS
BOX OFFICE POISON
NOMINATED FOR NOBEL
ALL CHARCTERS ©1998 THEIR RESPECTIVE CREATORS

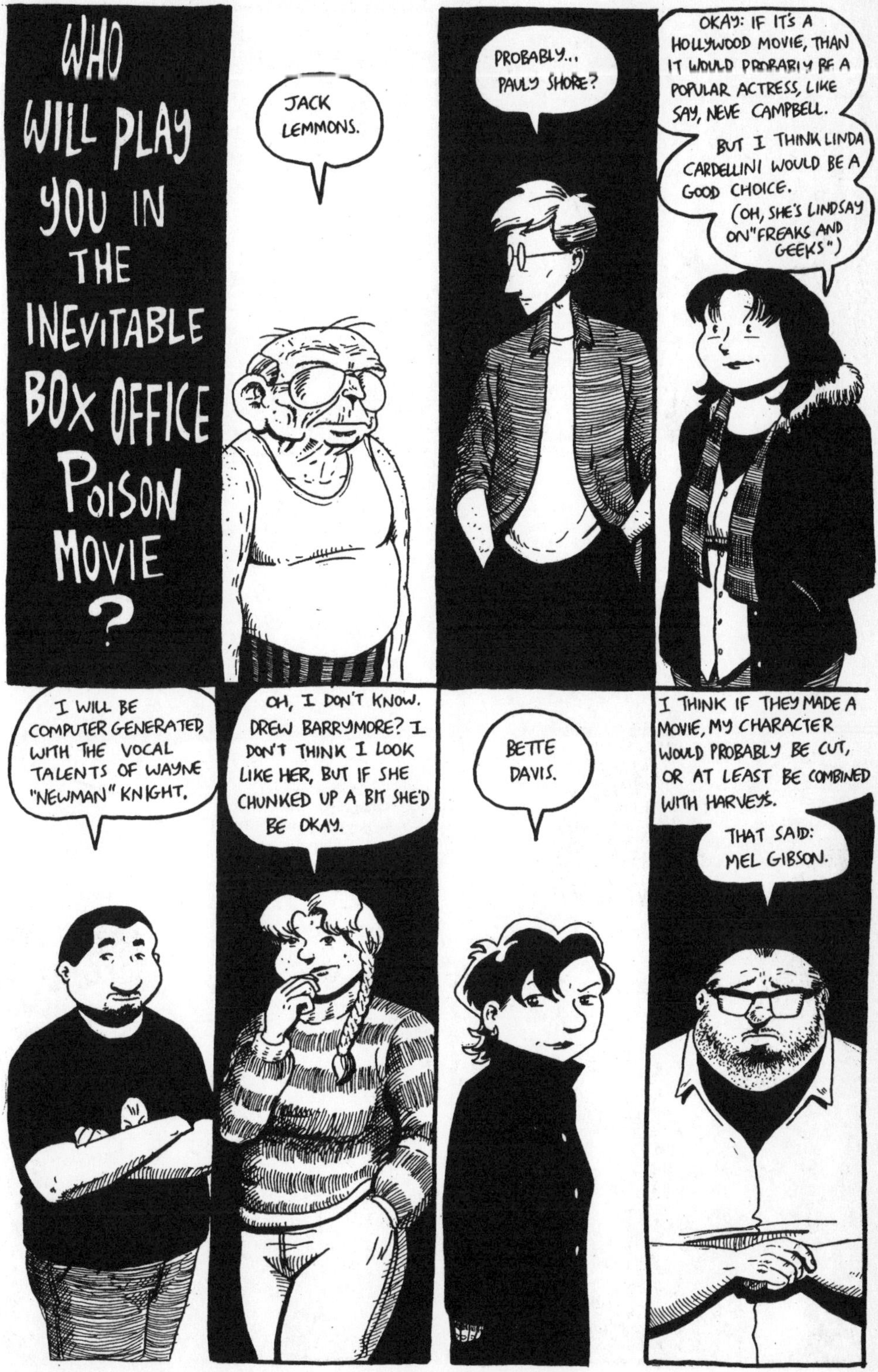
WHO WILL PLAY YOU IN THE INEVITABLE BOX OFFICE POISON MOVIE?
JACK LEMMONS.
PROBABLY... PAULY SHORE?
OKAY: IF IT'S A HOLLYWOOD MOVIE, THAN IT WOULD PROBABLY BE A POPULAR ACTRESS, LIKE SAY, NEVE CAMPBELL.
BUT I THINK LINDA CARDELLINI WOULD BE A GOOD CHOICE.
(OH, SHE'S LINDSAY ON "FREAKS AND GEEKS")
I WILL BE COMPUTER GENERATED, WITH THE VOCAL TALENTS OF WAYNE "NEWMAN" KNIGHT.
OH, I DON'T KNOW. DREW BARRYMORE? I DON'T THINK I LOOK LIKE HER, BUT IF SHE CHUNKED UP A BIT SHE'D BE OKAY.
BETTE DAVIS.
I THINK IF THEY MADE A MOVIE, MY CHARACTER WOULD PROBABLY BE CUT, OR AT LEAST BE COMBINED WITH HARVEY'S.
THAT SAID: MEL GIBSON.

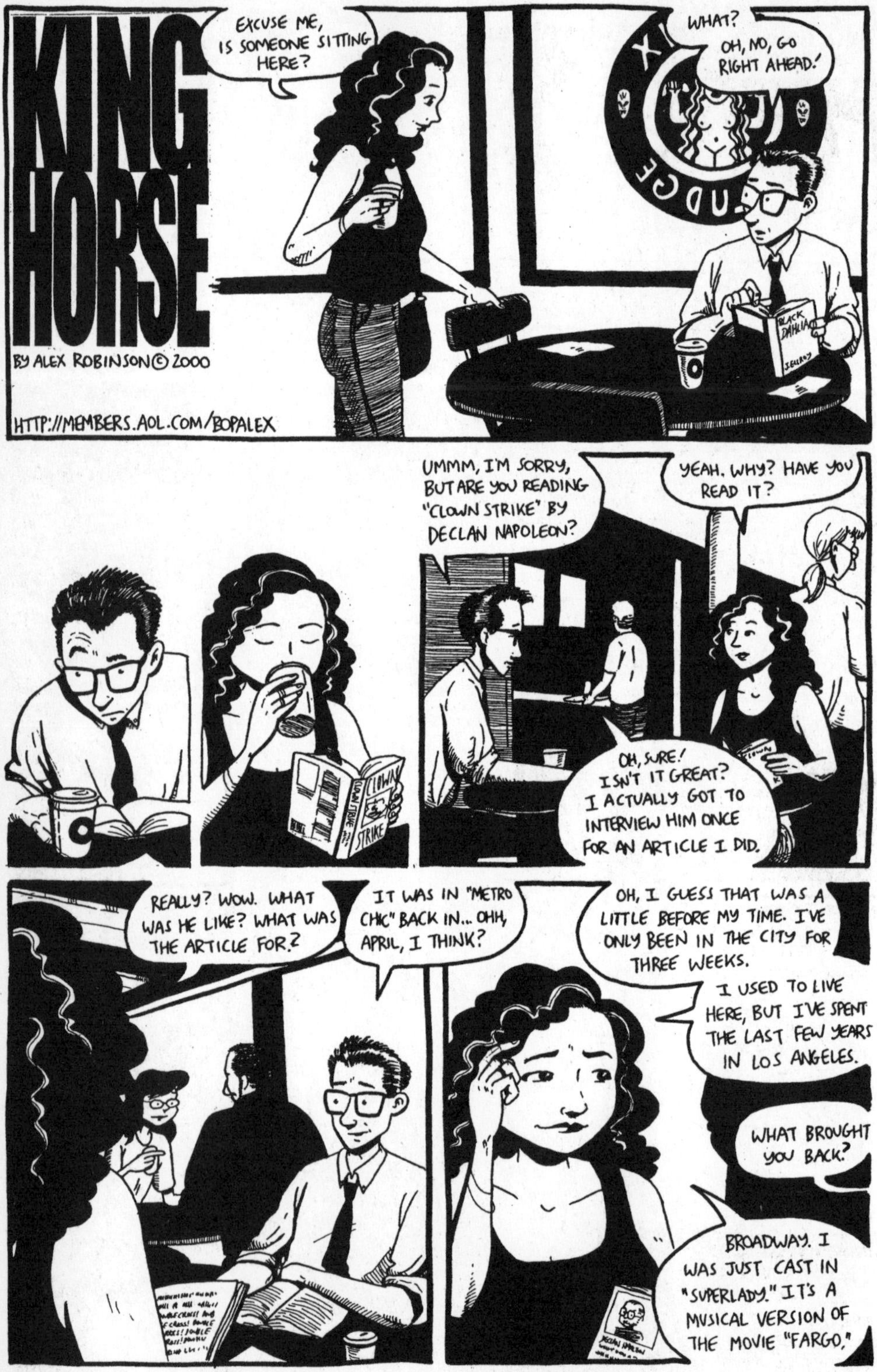
KING HORSE
BY ALEX ROBINSON © 2000
HTTP://MEMBERS.AOL.COM/BOPALEX
EXCUSE ME, IS SOMEONE SITTING HERE?
WHAT?
OH, NO, GO RIGHT AHEAD!
BLACK DAHLIA
J. ELLROY
CLOWN STRIKE
UMMM, I'M SORRY, BUT ARE YOU READING "CLOWN STRIKE" BY DECLAN NAPOLEON?
YEAH. WHY? HAVE YOU READ IT?
OH, SURE! ISN'T IT GREAT? I ACTUALLY GOT TO INTERVIEW HIM ONCE FOR AN ARTICLE I DID.
REALLY? WOW. WHAT WAS HE LIKE? WHAT WAS THE ARTICLE FOR?
IT WAS IN "METRO CHIC" BACK IN... OHH, APRIL, I THINK?
OH, I GUESS THAT WAS A LITTLE BEFORE MY TIME. I'VE ONLY BEEN IN THE CITY FOR THREE WEEKS.
I USED TO LIVE HERE, BUT I'VE SPENT THE LAST FEW YEARS IN LOS ANGELES.
WHAT BROUGHT YOU BACK?
BROADWAY. I WAS JUST CAST IN "SUPERLADY." IT'S A MUSICAL VERSION OF THE MOVIE "FARGO."

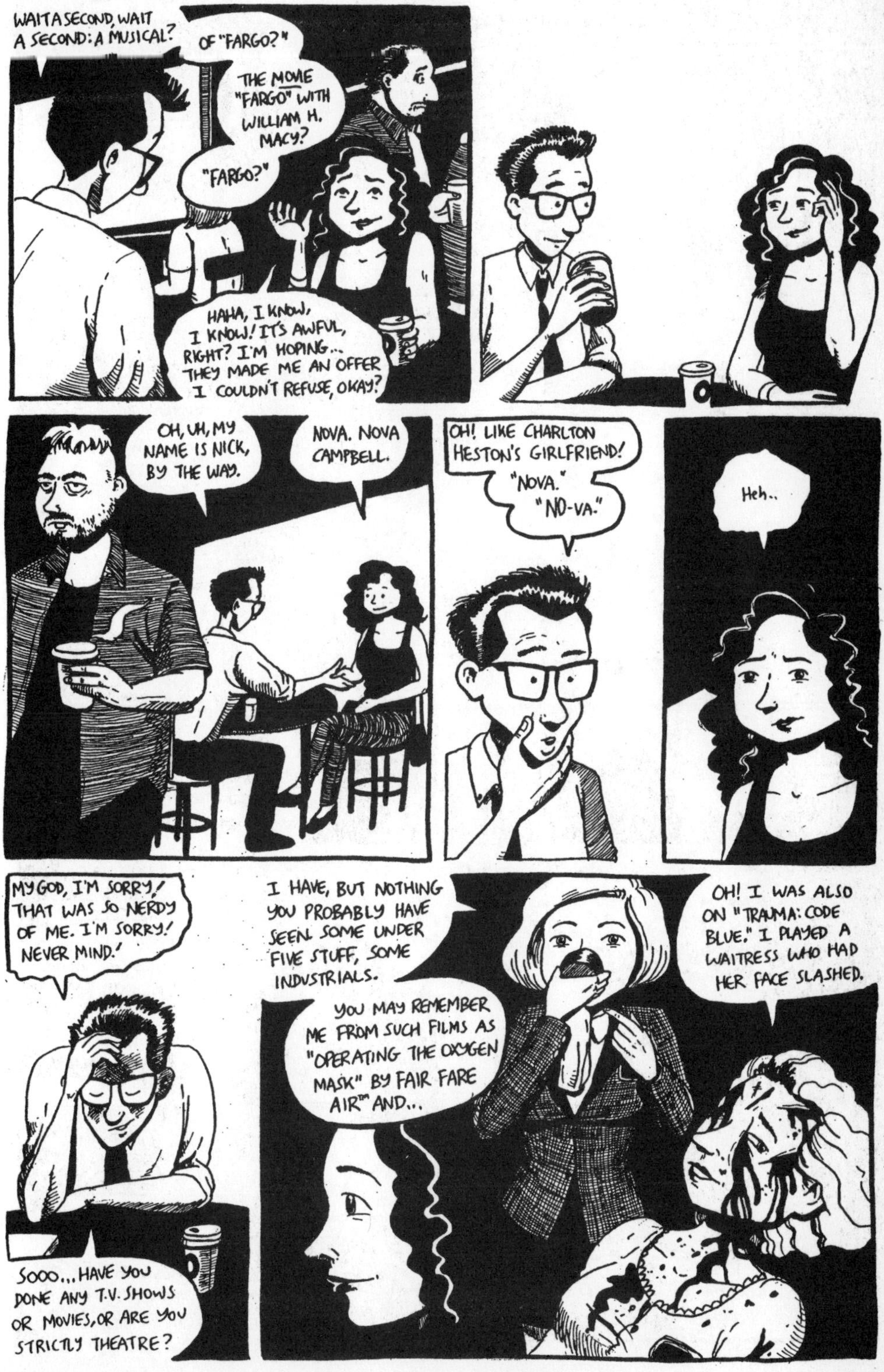
WAIT A SECOND, WAIT A SECOND: A MUSICAL?
OF "FARGO?"
THE MOVIE "FARGO" WITH WILLIAM H. MACY?
"FARGO?"
HAHA, I KNOW, I KNOW! IT'S AWFUL, RIGHT? I'M HOPING... THEY MADE ME AN OFFER I COULDN'T REFUSE, OKAY?
OH, UH, MY NAME IS NICK, BY THE WAY.
NOVA. NOVA CAMPBELL.
OH! LIKE CHARLTON HESTON'S GIRLFRIEND!
"NOVA."
"NO-VA."
Heh..
MY GOD, I'M SORRY! THAT WAS SO NERDY OF ME. I'M SORRY! NEVER MIND!
SOOO... HAVE YOU DONE ANY T.V. SHOWS OR MOVIES, OR ARE YOU STRICTLY THEATRE?
I HAVE, BUT NOTHING YOU PROBABLY HAVE SEEN. SOME UNDER FIVE STUFF, SOME INDUSTRIALS.
YOU MAY REMEMBER ME FROM SUCH FILMS AS "OPERATING THE OXYGEN MASK" BY FAIR FARE AIR™ AND...
OH! I WAS ALSO ON "TRAUMA: CODE BLUE." I PLAYED A WAITRESS WHO HAD HER FACE SLASHED.

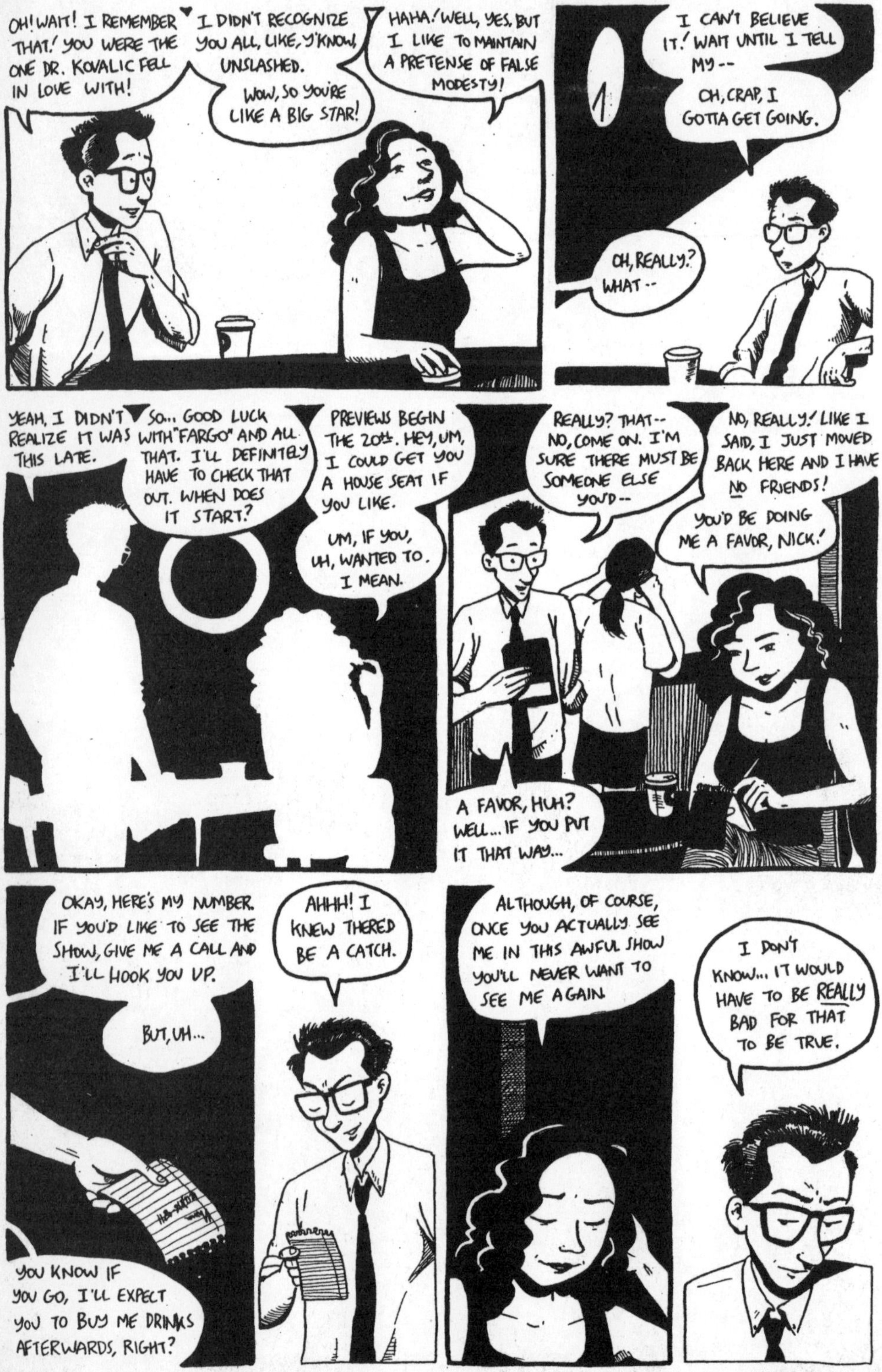
OH! WAIT! I REMEMBER THAT! YOU WERE THE ONE DR. KOVALIC FELL IN LOVE WITH!
I DIDN'T RECOGNIZE YOU ALL, LIKE, Y'KNOW, UNSLASHED.
WOW, SO YOU'RE LIKE A BIG STAR!
HAHA! WELL, YES. BUT I LIKE TO MAINTAIN A PRETENSE OF FALSE MODESTY!
I CAN'T BELIEVE IT! WAIT UNTIL I TELL MY --
OH, CRAP, I GOTTA GET GOING.
OH, REALLY? WHAT --
YEAH, I DIDN'T REALIZE IT WAS THIS LATE.
SO... GOOD LUCK WITH "FARGO" AND ALL THAT. I'LL DEFINITELY HAVE TO CHECK THAT OUT. WHEN DOES IT START?
PREVIEWS BEGIN THE 20TH. HEY, UM, I COULD GET YOU A HOUSE SEAT IF YOU LIKE.
UM, IF YOU, UH, WANTED TO. I MEAN.
REALLY? THAT-- NO, COME ON. I'M SURE THERE MUST BE SOMEONE ELSE YOU'D --
NO, REALLY! LIKE I SAID, I JUST MOVED BACK HERE AND I HAVE NO FRIENDS!
YOU'D BE DOING ME A FAVOR, NICK!
A FAVOR, HUH? WELL... IF YOU PUT IT THAT WAY...
OKAY, HERE'S MY NUMBER. IF YOU'D LIKE TO SEE THE SHOW, GIVE ME A CALL AND I'LL HOOK YOU UP.
BUT, UH...
YOU KNOW IF YOU GO, I'LL EXPECT YOU TO BUY ME DRINKS AFTERWARDS, RIGHT?
AHHH! I KNEW THERE'D BE A CATCH.
ALTHOUGH, OF COURSE, ONCE YOU ACTUALLY SEE ME IN THIS AWFUL SHOW YOU'LL NEVER WANT TO SEE ME AGAIN.
I DON'T KNOW... IT WOULD HAVE TO BE REALLY BAD FOR THAT TO BE TRUE.

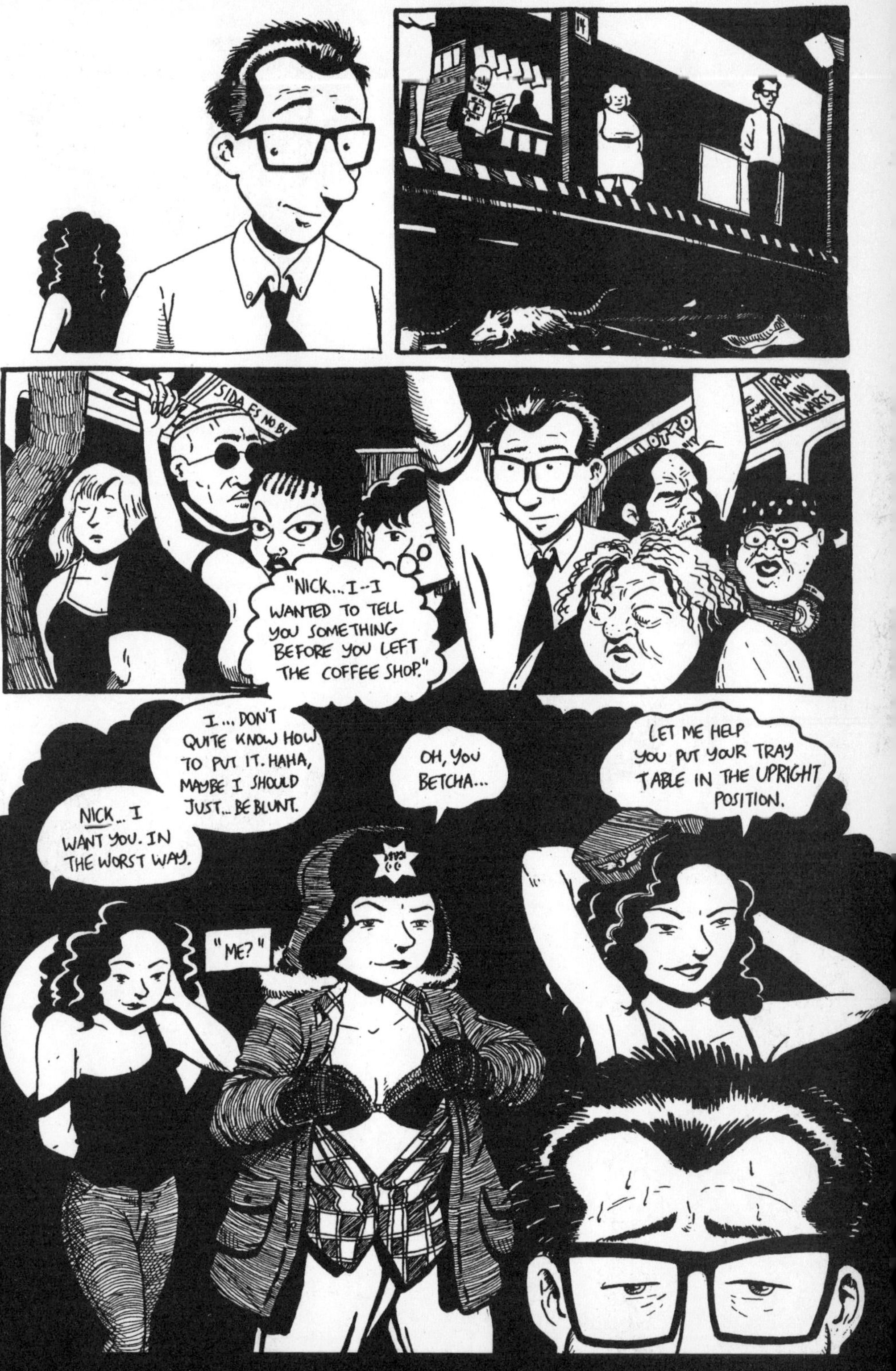

SIDA ES NO B
"NICK... I--I WANTED TO TELL YOU SOMETHING BEFORE YOU LEFT THE COFFEE SHOP."
I... DON'T QUITE KNOW HOW TO PUT IT. HAHA, MAYBE I SHOULD JUST... BE BLUNT.
NICK... I WANT YOU. IN THE WORST WAY.
"ME?"
OH, YOU BETCHA...
LET ME HELP YOU PUT YOUR TRAY TABLE IN THE UPRIGHT POSITION.

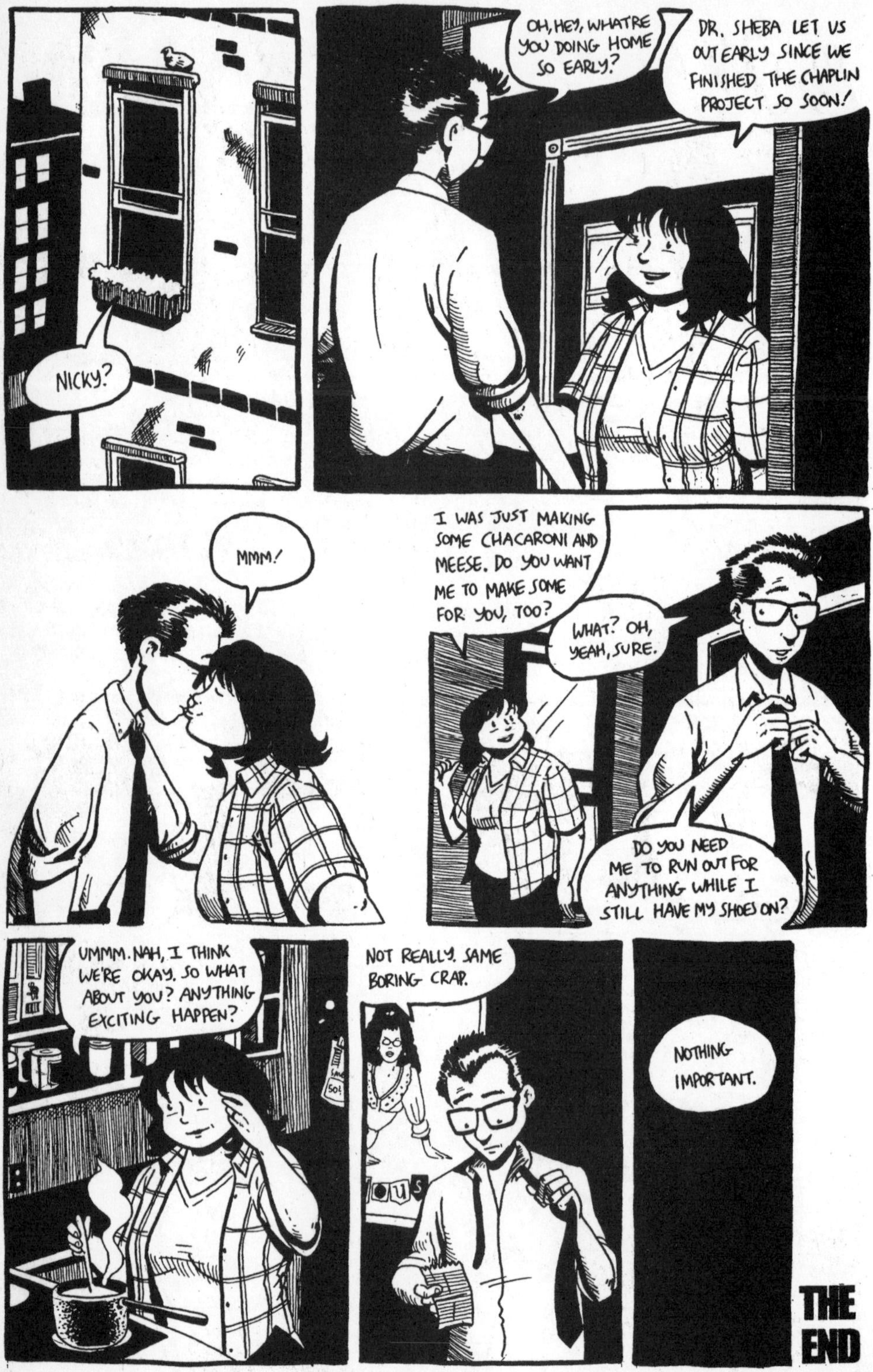
NICKY?
OH, HEY, WHATRE YOU DOING HOME SO EARLY?
DR. SHEBA LET US OUT EARLY SINCE WE FINISHED THE CHAPLIN PROJECT SO SOON!
MMM!
I WAS JUST MAKING SOME CHACARONI AND MEESE. DO YOU WANT ME TO MAKE SOME FOR YOU, TOO?
WHAT? OH, YEAH, SURE.
DO YOU NEED ME TO RUN OUT FOR ANYTHING WHILE I STILL HAVE MY SHOES ON?
UMMM. NAH, I THINK WE'RE OKAY. SO WHAT ABOUT YOU? ANYTHING EXCITING HAPPEN?
NOT REALLY. SAME BORING CRAP.
NOTHING IMPORTANT.
THE END

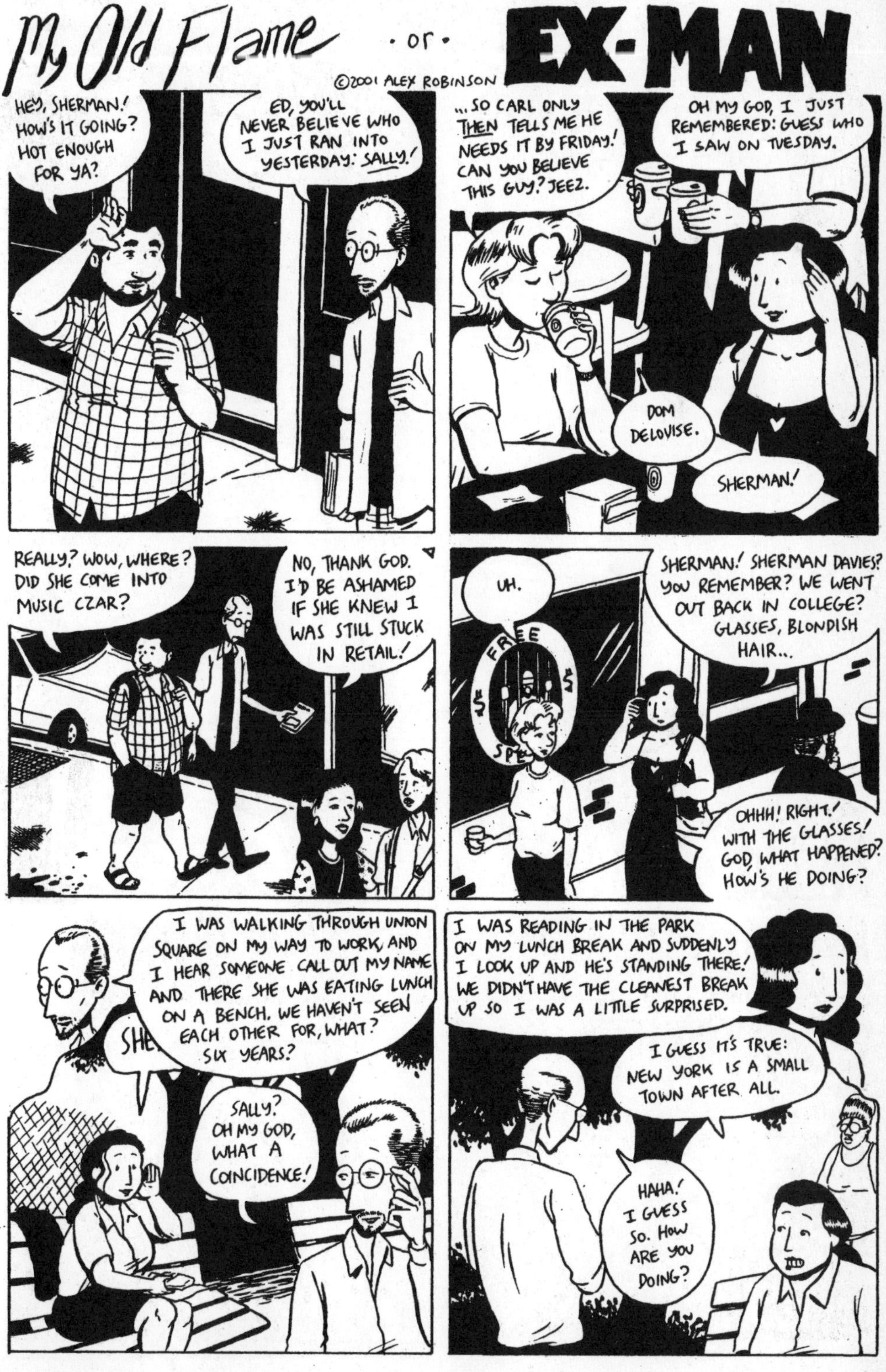
My Old Flame · or · EX-MAN
©2001 ALEX ROBINSON
HEY, SHERMAN! HOW'S IT GOING? HOT ENOUGH FOR YA?
ED, YOU'LL NEVER BELIEVE WHO I JUST RAN INTO YESTERDAY: SALLY!
...SO CARL ONLY THEN TELLS ME HE NEEDS IT BY FRIDAY! CAN YOU BELIEVE THIS GUY? JEEZ.
OH MY GOD, I JUST REMEMBERED: GUESS WHO I SAW ON TUESDAY.
DOM DELOUISE.
SHERMAN!
REALLY? WOW, WHERE? DID SHE COME INTO MUSIC CZAR?
NO, THANK GOD. I'D BE ASHAMED IF SHE KNEW I WAS STILL STUCK IN RETAIL!
UH.
FREE
SHERMAN! SHERMAN DAVIES? YOU REMEMBER? WE WENT OUT BACK IN COLLEGE? GLASSES, BLONDISH HAIR...
OHHH! RIGHT! WITH THE GLASSES! GOD, WHAT HAPPENED? HOW'S HE DOING?
I WAS WALKING THROUGH UNION SQUARE ON MY WAY TO WORK, AND I HEAR SOMEONE CALL OUT MY NAME AND THERE SHE WAS EATING LUNCH ON A BENCH. WE HAVEN'T SEEN EACH OTHER FOR, WHAT? SIX YEARS?
SALLY? OH MY GOD, WHAT A COINCIDENCE!
I WAS READING IN THE PARK ON MY LUNCH BREAK AND SUDDENLY I LOOK UP AND HE'S STANDING THERE! WE DIDN'T HAVE THE CLEANEST BREAK UP SO I WAS A LITTLE SURPRISED.
I GUESS IT'S TRUE: NEW YORK IS A SMALL TOWN AFTER ALL.
HAHA! I GUESS SO. HOW ARE YOU DOING?

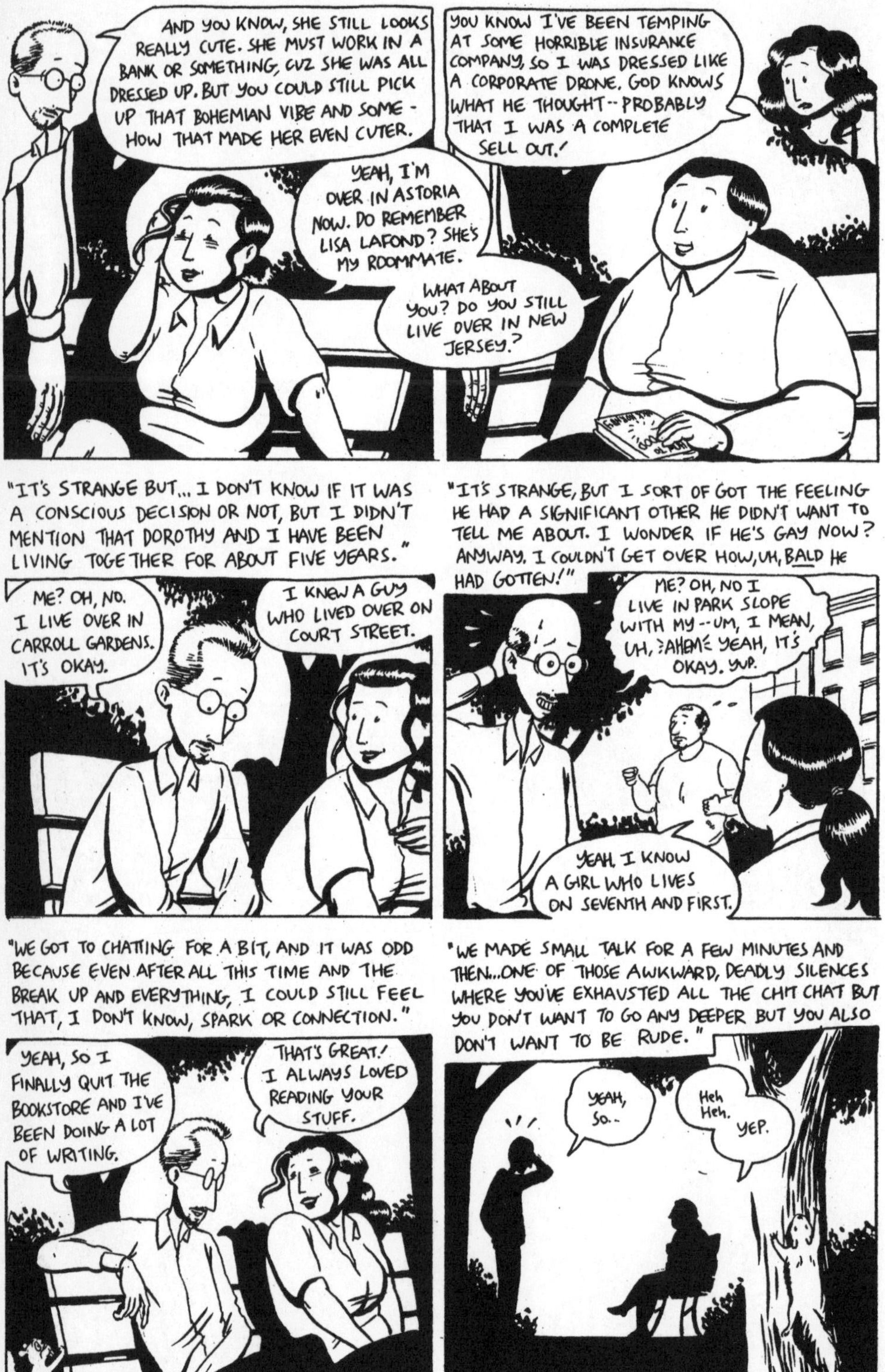
AND YOU KNOW, SHE STILL LOOKS REALLY CUTE. SHE MUST WORK IN A BANK OR SOMETHING, CUZ SHE WAS ALL DRESSED UP. BUT YOU COULD STILL PICK UP THAT BOHEMIAN VIBE AND SOME-HOW THAT MADE HER EVEN CUTER.
YEAH, I'M OVER IN ASTORIA NOW. DO REMEMBER LISA LAFOND? SHE'S MY ROOMMATE.
YOU KNOW I'VE BEEN TEMPING AT SOME HORRIBLE INSURANCE COMPANY, SO I WAS DRESSED LIKE A CORPORATE DRONE. GOD KNOWS WHAT HE THOUGHT-- PROBABLY THAT I WAS A COMPLETE SELL OUT!
WHAT ABOUT YOU? DO YOU STILL LIVE OVER IN NEW JERSEY?
"IT'S STRANGE BUT... I DON'T KNOW IF IT WAS A CONSCIOUS DECISION OR NOT, BUT I DIDN'T MENTION THAT DOROTHY AND I HAVE BEEN LIVING TOGETHER FOR ABOUT FIVE YEARS."
"IT'S STRANGE, BUT I SORT OF GOT THE FEELING HE HAD A SIGNIFICANT OTHER HE DIDN'T WANT TO TELL ME ABOUT. I WONDER IF HE'S GAY NOW? ANYWAY, I COULDN'T GET OVER HOW, UH, BALD HE HAD GOTTEN!"
ME? OH, NO. I LIVE OVER IN CARROLL GARDENS. IT'S OKAY.
I KNEW A GUY WHO LIVED OVER ON COURT STREET.
ME? OH, NO I LIVE IN PARK SLOPE WITH MY-- UM, I MEAN, UH, AHEM YEAH, IT'S OKAY. YUP.
YEAH, I KNOW A GIRL WHO LIVES ON SEVENTH AND FIRST.
"WE GOT TO CHATTING FOR A BIT, AND IT WAS ODD BECAUSE EVEN AFTER ALL THIS TIME AND THE BREAK UP AND EVERYTHING, I COULD STILL FEEL THAT, I DON'T KNOW, SPARK OR CONNECTION."
"WE MADE SMALL TALK FOR A FEW MINUTES AND THEN...ONE OF THOSE AWKWARD, DEADLY SILENCES WHERE YOU'VE EXHAUSTED ALL THE CHIT CHAT BUT YOU DON'T WANT TO GO ANY DEEPER BUT YOU ALSO DON'T WANT TO BE RUDE."
YEAH, SO I FINALLY QUIT THE BOOKSTORE AND I'VE BEEN DOING A LOT OF WRITING.
THAT'S GREAT! I ALWAYS LOVED READING YOUR STUFF.
YEAH, SO..
Heh Heh. YEP.

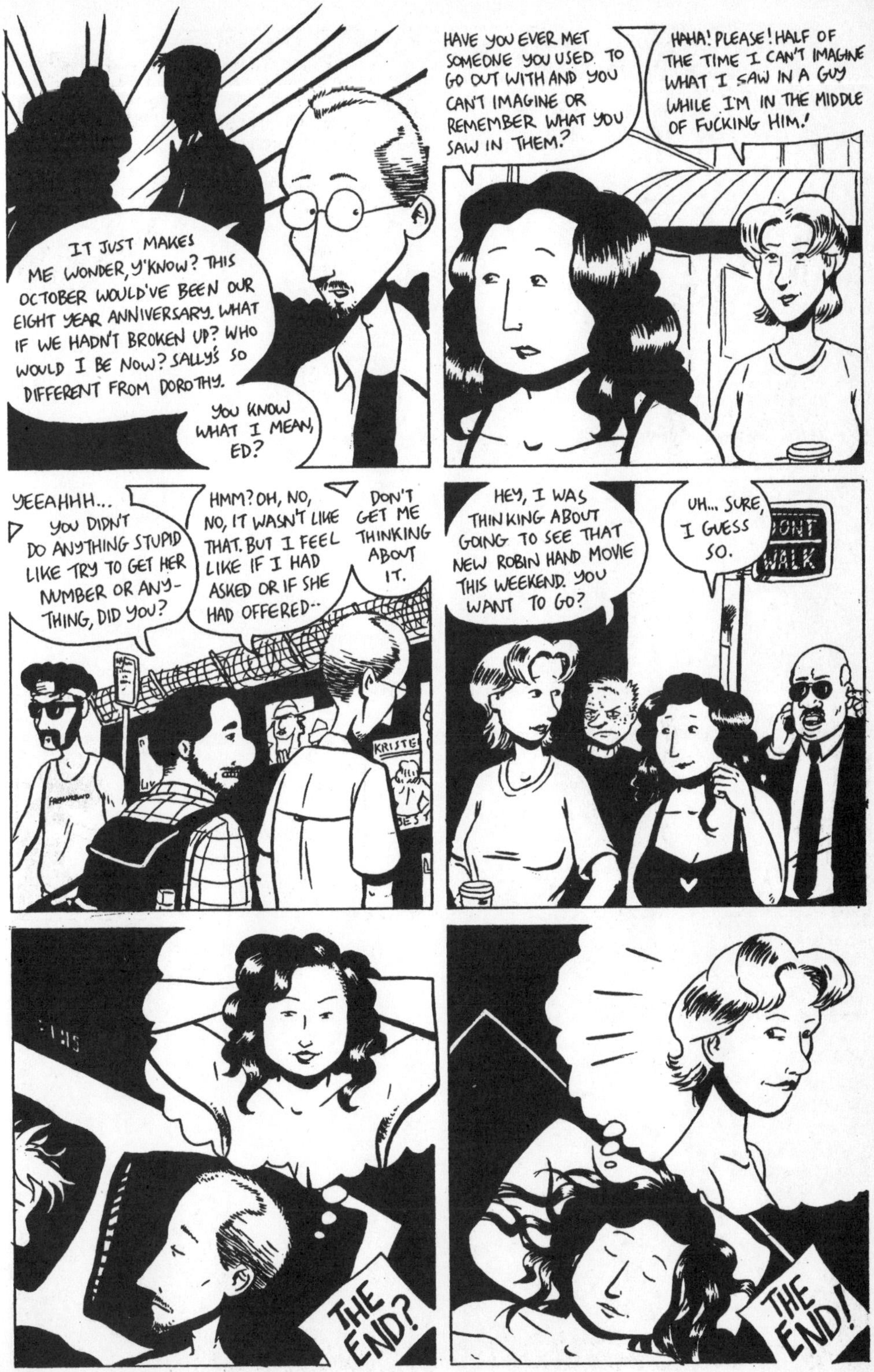
IT JUST MAKES ME WONDER, Y'KNOW? THIS OCTOBER WOULD'VE BEEN OUR EIGHT YEAR ANNIVERSARY. WHAT IF WE HADN'T BROKEN UP? WHO WOULD I BE NOW? SALLY'S SO DIFFERENT FROM DOROTHY.
YOU KNOW WHAT I MEAN, ED?
HAVE YOU EVER MET SOMEONE YOU USED TO GO OUT WITH AND YOU CAN'T IMAGINE OR REMEMBER WHAT YOU SAW IN THEM?
HAHA! PLEASE! HALF OF THE TIME I CAN'T IMAGINE WHAT I SAW IN A GUY WHILE I'M IN THE MIDDLE OF FUCKING HIM!
YEEAHHH... YOU DIDN'T DO ANYTHING STUPID LIKE TRY TO GET HER NUMBER OR ANY-THING, DID YOU?
HMM? OH, NO, NO, IT WASN'T LIKE THAT. BUT I FEEL LIKE IF I HAD ASKED OR IF SHE HAD OFFERED--
DON'T GET ME THINKING ABOUT IT.
HEY, I WAS THINKING ABOUT GOING TO SEE THAT NEW ROBIN HAND MOVIE THIS WEEKEND. YOU WANT TO GO?
UH... SURE, I GUESS SO.
DONT WALK
THE END?
THE END!

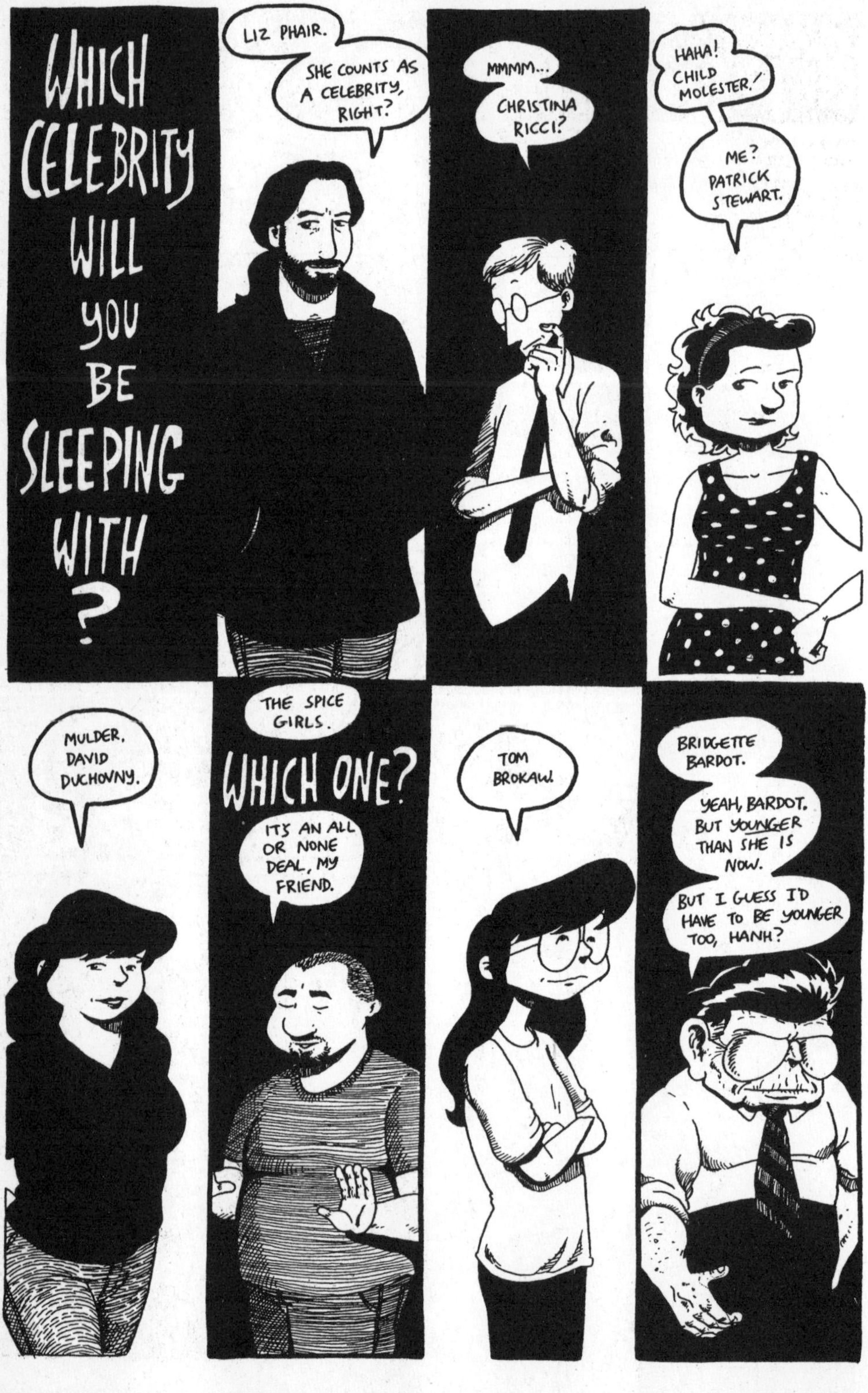
WHICH CELEBRITY WILL YOU BE SLEEPING WITH ?
LIZ PHAIR.
SHE COUNTS AS A CELEBRITY, RIGHT?
MMMM...
CHRISTINA RICCI?
HAHA! CHILD MOLESTER!
ME? PATRICK STEWART.
MULDER. DAVID DUCHOVNY.
THE SPICE GIRLS.
WHICH ONE?
IT'S AN ALL OR NONE DEAL, MY FRIEND.
TOM BROKAW!
BRIDGETTE BARDOT.
YEAH, BARDOT. BUT YOUNGER THAN SHE IS NOW.
BUT I GUESS I'D HAVE TO BE YOUNGER TOO, HANH?

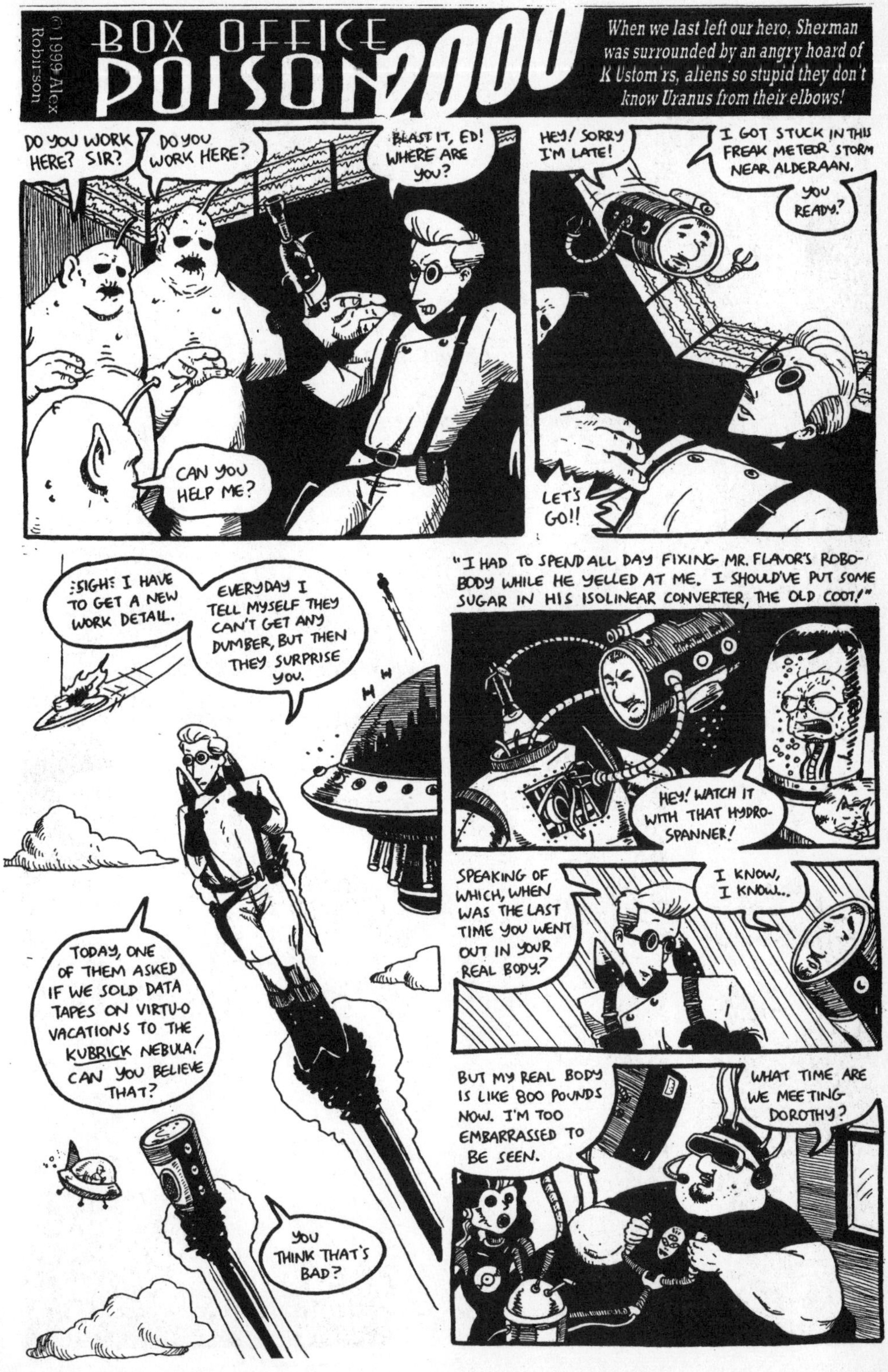
©1999 Alex Robinson
BOX OFFICE POISON 2000
When we last left our hero, Sherman was surrounded by an angry hoard of K Ustom'rs, aliens so stupid they don't know Uranus from their elbows!
DO YOU WORK HERE? SIR?
DO YOU WORK HERE?
BLAST IT, ED! WHERE ARE YOU?
CAN YOU HELP ME?
HEY! SORRY I'M LATE!
I GOT STUCK IN THIS FREAK METEOR STORM NEAR ALDERAAN.
YOU READY?
LET'S GO!!
:SIGH: I HAVE TO GET A NEW WORK DETAIL.
EVERYDAY I TELL MYSELF THEY CAN'T GET ANY DUMBER, BUT THEN THEY SURPRISE YOU.
TODAY, ONE OF THEM ASKED IF WE SOLD DATA TAPES ON VIRTU-O VACATIONS TO THE KUBRICK NEBULA! CAN YOU BELIEVE THAT?
YOU THINK THAT'S BAD?
"I HAD TO SPEND ALL DAY FIXING MR. FLAVOR'S ROBO-BODY WHILE HE YELLED AT ME. I SHOULD'VE PUT SOME SUGAR IN HIS ISOLINEAR CONVERTER, THE OLD COOT!"
HEY! WATCH IT WITH THAT HYDRO-SPANNER!
SPEAKING OF WHICH, WHEN WAS THE LAST TIME YOU WENT OUT IN YOUR REAL BODY?
I KNOW, I KNOW...
BUT MY REAL BODY IS LIKE 800 POUNDS NOW. I'M TOO EMBARRASSED TO BE SEEN.
WHAT TIME ARE WE MEETING DOROTHY?

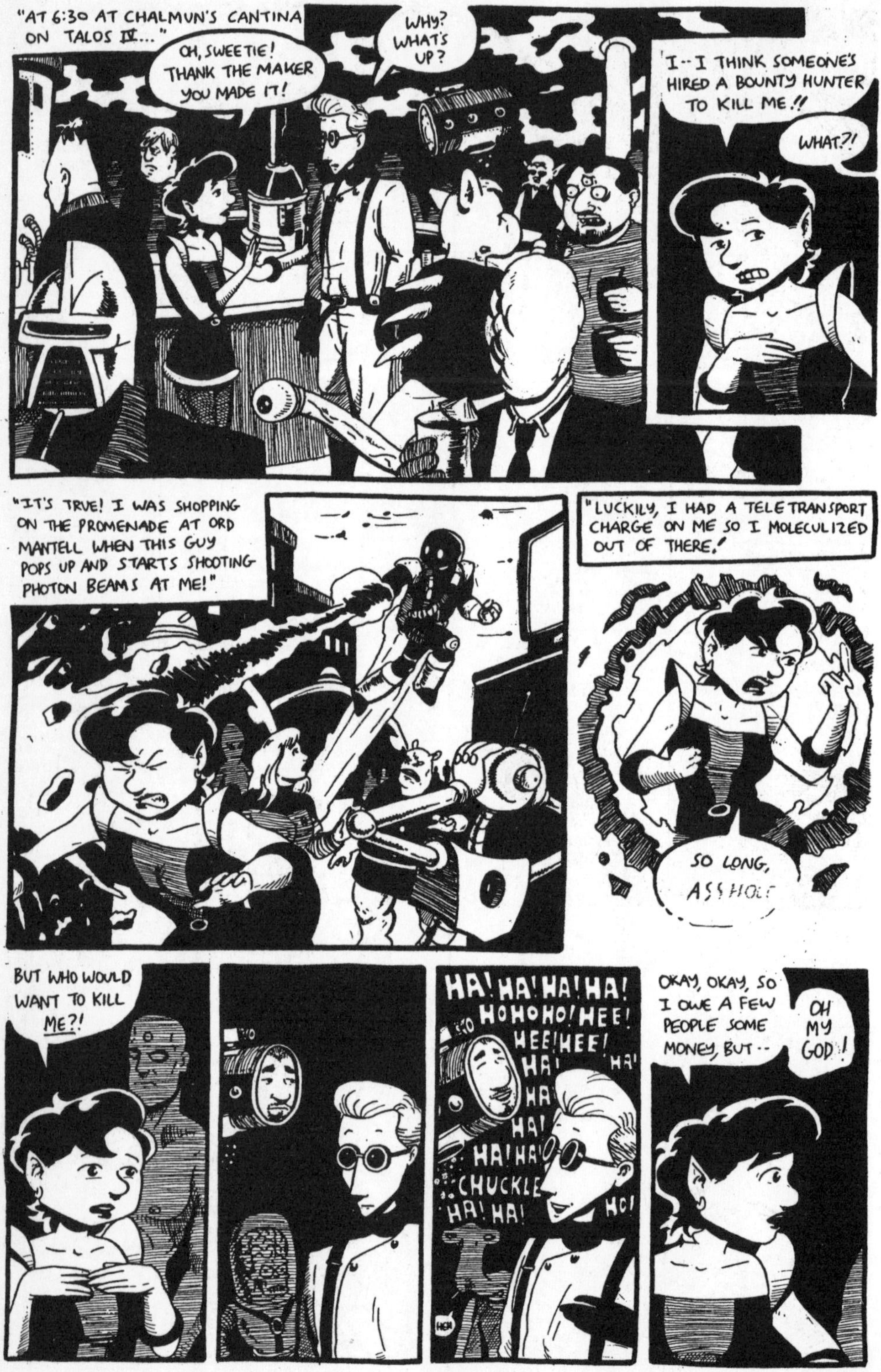
"AT 6:30 AT CHALMUN'S CANTINA ON TALOS IV..."
OH, SWEETIE! THANK THE MAKER YOU MADE IT!
WHY? WHAT'S UP?
I-- I THINK SOMEONE'S HIRED A BOUNTY HUNTER TO KILL ME!!
WHAT?!
"IT'S TRUE! I WAS SHOPPING ON THE PROMENADE AT ORD MANTELL WHEN THIS GUY POPS UP AND STARTS SHOOTING PHOTON BEAMS AT ME!"
"LUCKILY, I HAD A TELETRANSPORT CHARGE ON ME SO I MOLECULIZED OUT OF THERE!
SO LONG,
BUT WHO WOULD WANT TO KILL ME?!
HA! HA! HA! HA! HOHOHO! HEE! HEE! HEE! HA! HA HA HA! HA! HA! HA! CHUCKLE HA! HA! HO! HEH
OKAY, OKAY, SO I OWE A FEW PEOPLE SOME MONEY, BUT --
OH MY GOD!

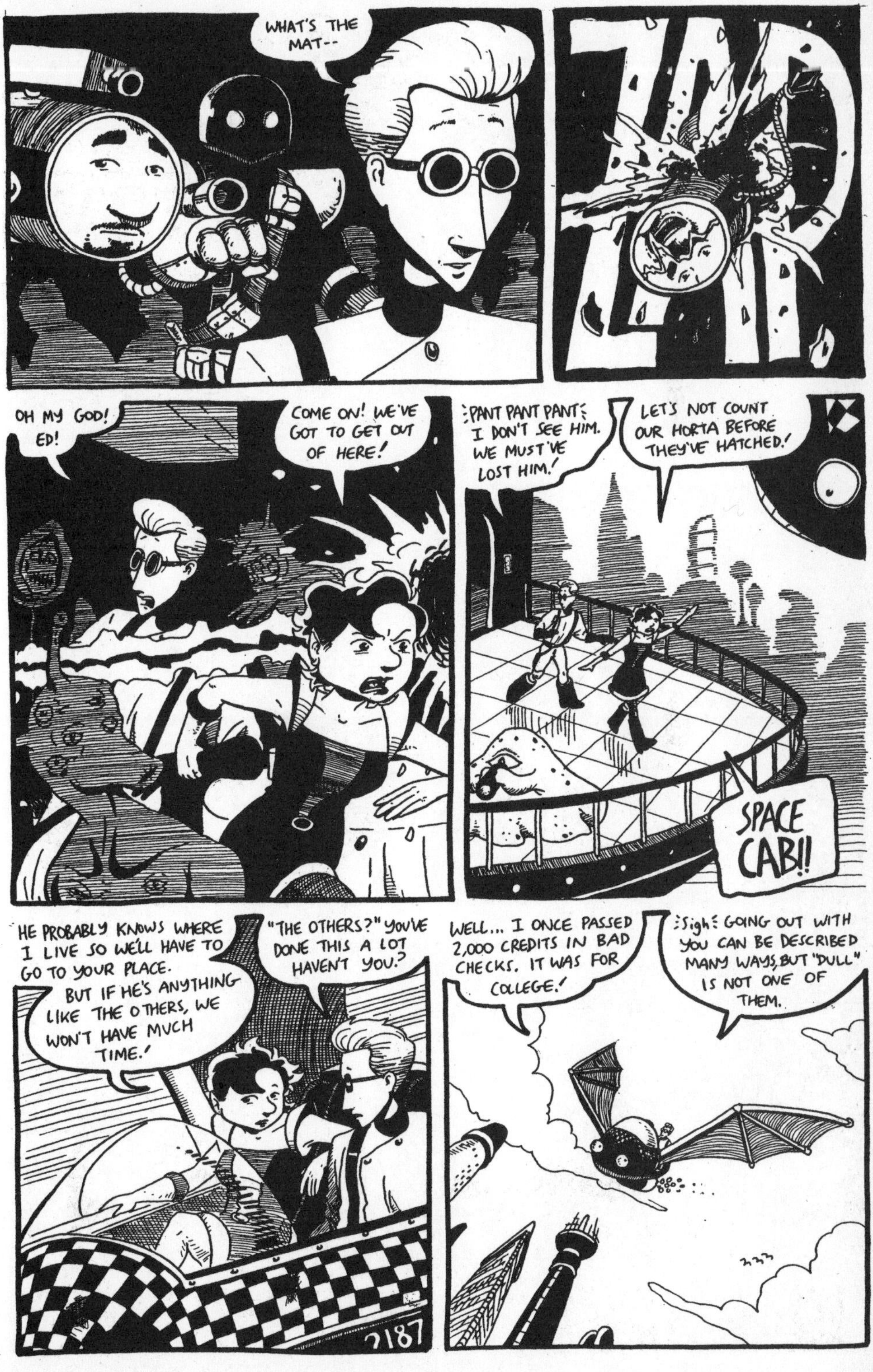
WHAT'S THE MAT--
OH MY GOD! ED!
COME ON! WE'VE GOT TO GET OUT OF HERE!
PANT PANT PANT I DON'T SEE HIM. WE MUST'VE LOST HIM!
LET'S NOT COUNT OUR HORTA BEFORE THEY'VE HATCHED!
SPACE CAB!!
HE PROBABLY KNOWS WHERE I LIVE SO WE'LL HAVE TO GO TO YOUR PLACE.
BUT IF HE'S ANYTHING LIKE THE OTHERS, WE WON'T HAVE MUCH TIME!
"THE OTHERS?" YOU'VE DONE THIS A LOT HAVEN'T YOU?
2187
WELL... I ONCE PASSED 2,000 CREDITS IN BAD CHECKS. IT WAS FOR COLLEGE!
SIGH GOING OUT WITH YOU CAN BE DESCRIBED MANY WAYS, BUT "DULL" IS NOT ONE OF THEM.

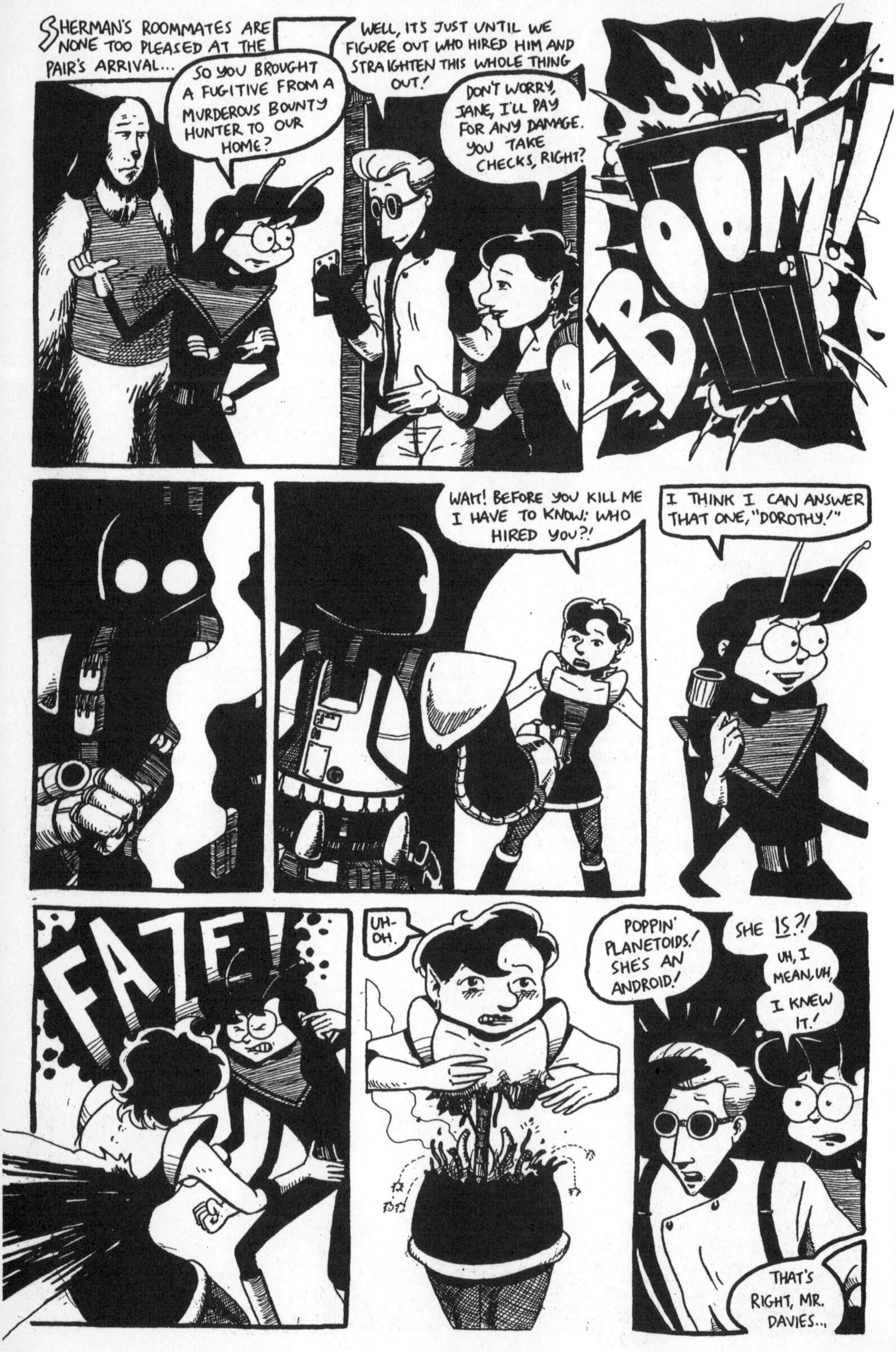
SHERMAN'S ROOMMATES ARE NONE TOO PLEASED AT THE PAIR'S ARRIVAL...
SO YOU BROUGHT A FUGITIVE FROM A MURDEROUS BOUNTY HUNTER TO OUR HOME?
WELL, IT'S JUST UNTIL WE FIGURE OUT WHO HIRED HIM AND STRAIGHTEN THIS WHOLE THING OUT!
DON'T WORRY, JANE, I'LL PAY FOR ANY DAMAGE. YOU TAKE CHECKS, RIGHT?
BOOM!
WAIT! BEFORE YOU KILL ME I HAVE TO KNOW: WHO HIRED YOU?!
I THINK I CAN ANSWER THAT ONE, "DOROTHY!"
FAZE!
UH-OH.
POPPIN' PLANETOIDS! SHE'S AN ANDROID!
SHE IS?!
UH, I MEAN, UH, I KNEW IT!
THAT'S RIGHT, MR. DAVIES...

I'M AFRAID YOU'VE ALL BEEN THE VICTIM OF A TERRIBLE HOAX!

WHAT TH--?!

"YOU SEE, I CREATED THIS ROBOT TO HELP ME CATALOG MY MASSIVE PERSONAL LIBRARY-- OVER 39,000 VOLUMES-- ON PRAXIS-9. DESPITE MY MASSIVE PERSONAL FORTUNE -- OVER 2.8 TRILLION CREDITS-- I BUILT IT USING KNOCK-OFF, BOOTLEGGED SOFTWARE."

"HERE'S WHERE MY TROUBLES BEGAN."

"INSTEAD OF BEING KIND, RATIONAL AND ECONOMICAL, LIKE ITS CREATOR, THE ANDROID WAS A CYNICAL, HARD-DRINKING SPENDTHRIFT."

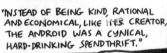

"LET THIS BE A LESSON TO YOU ALL ABOUT THE PERILS OF ILLEGAL SOFTWARE."

SCREW YOU, EGGHEAD!

"BEFORE I COULD SHUT IT DOWN, SHE RAN OFF. IT TOOK ME MONTHS TO TRACK IT DOWN."

JEEZ! I CAN'T BELIEVE I WAS HAVING SEX WITH A FREAKIN' ROBOT!!

I'M TERRIBLY SORRY, MR. DAVIES. SHE...

SHE MAY'VE BEEN A CHAINSMOKING, EVIL AUTOMATON, BUT SHE DID HAVE GOOD TASTE IN MEN FOLK.

HUH? WHAT DO YOU MEAN, GORGEOUS?

COME WITH ME TO PRAXIS-9, MR. DAVIES! HELP ME CATALOG MY BOOKS!

BUT WHAT ABOUT ME?!

NOW, LADIES! NOT BICKER! YOU BOTH HAVE ME...

MEANWHILE, BACK IN THE 20th CENTURY...

SWEETIE? I'M A LITTLE SHORT ON MY RENT THIS MONTH. CAN I BORROW...

END

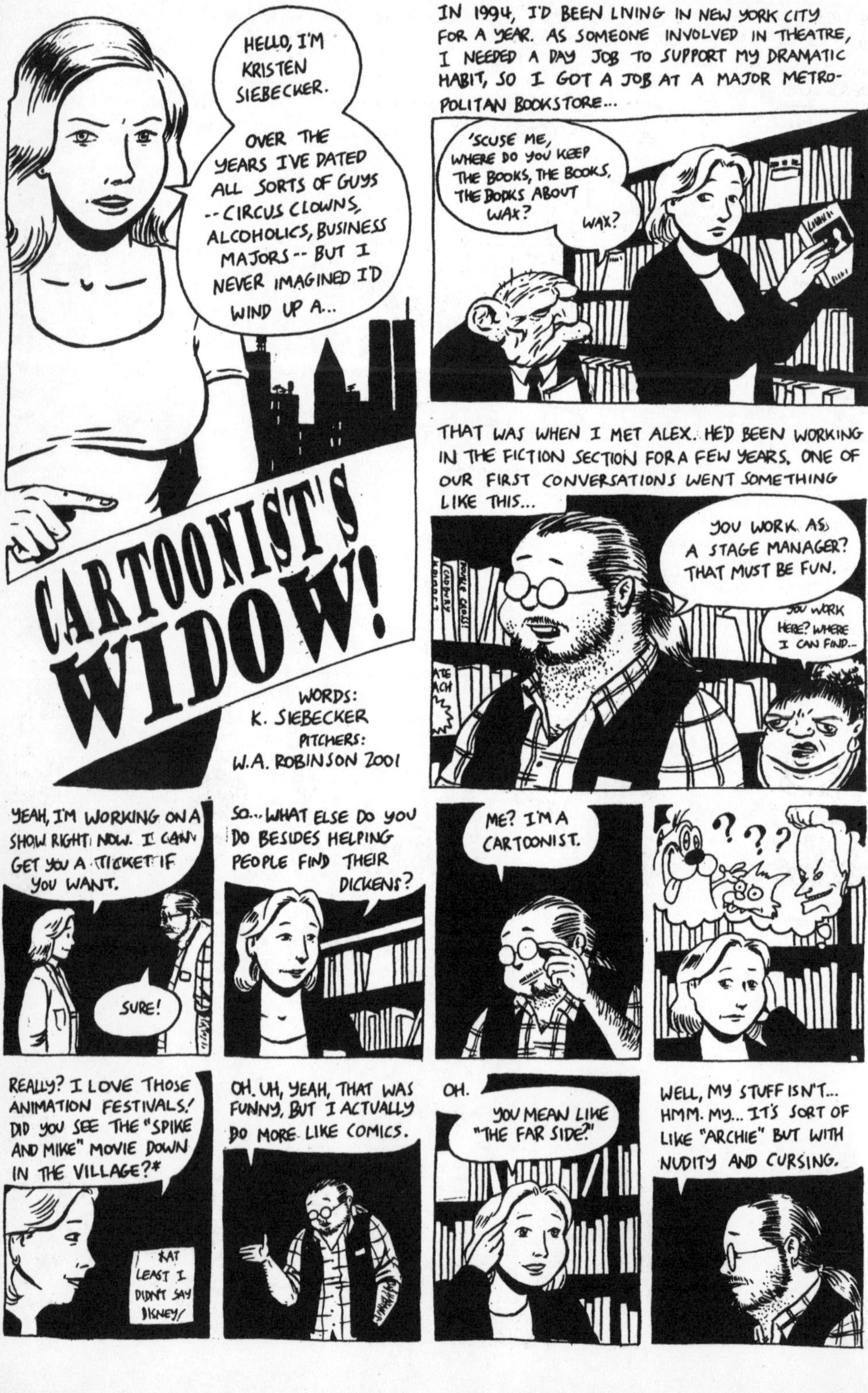
HELLO, I'M KRISTEN SIEBECKER.
OVER THE YEARS I'VE DATED ALL SORTS OF GUYS --CIRCUS CLOWNS, ALCOHOLICS, BUSINESS MAJORS-- BUT I NEVER IMAGINED I'D WIND UP A...
CARTOONIST'S WIDOW!
WORDS: K. SIEBECKER
PITCHERS: W.A. ROBINSON 2001
IN 1994, I'D BEEN LIVING IN NEW YORK CITY FOR A YEAR. AS SOMEONE INVOLVED IN THEATRE, I NEEDED A DAY JOB TO SUPPORT MY DRAMATIC HABIT, SO I GOT A JOB AT A MAJOR METRO-POLITAN BOOKSTORE...
'SCUSE ME, WHERE DO YOU KEEP THE BOOKS, THE BOOKS, THE BOOKS ABOUT WAX?
WAX?
THAT WAS WHEN I MET ALEX. HE'D BEEN WORKING IN THE FICTION SECTION FOR A FEW YEARS. ONE OF OUR FIRST CONVERSATIONS WENT SOMETHING LIKE THIS...
YOU WORK AS A STAGE MANAGER? THAT MUST BE FUN.
YOU WORK HERE? WHERE I CAN FIND...
YEAH, I'M WORKING ON A SHOW RIGHT NOW. I CAN GET YOU A TICKET IF YOU WANT.
SURE!
SO... WHAT ELSE DO YOU DO BESIDES HELPING PEOPLE FIND THEIR DICKENS?
ME? I'M A CARTOONIST.
???
REALLY? I LOVE THOSE ANIMATION FESTIVALS! DID YOU SEE THE "SPIKE AND MIKE" MOVIE DOWN IN THE VILLAGE?*
*AT LEAST I DIDN'T SAY DISNEY!
OH. UH, YEAH, THAT WAS FUNNY, BUT I ACTUALLY DO MORE LIKE COMICS.
OH.
YOU MEAN LIKE "THE FAR SIDE?"
WELL, MY STUFF ISN'T... HMM. MY... IT'S SORT OF LIKE "ARCHIE" BUT WITH NUDITY AND CURSING.

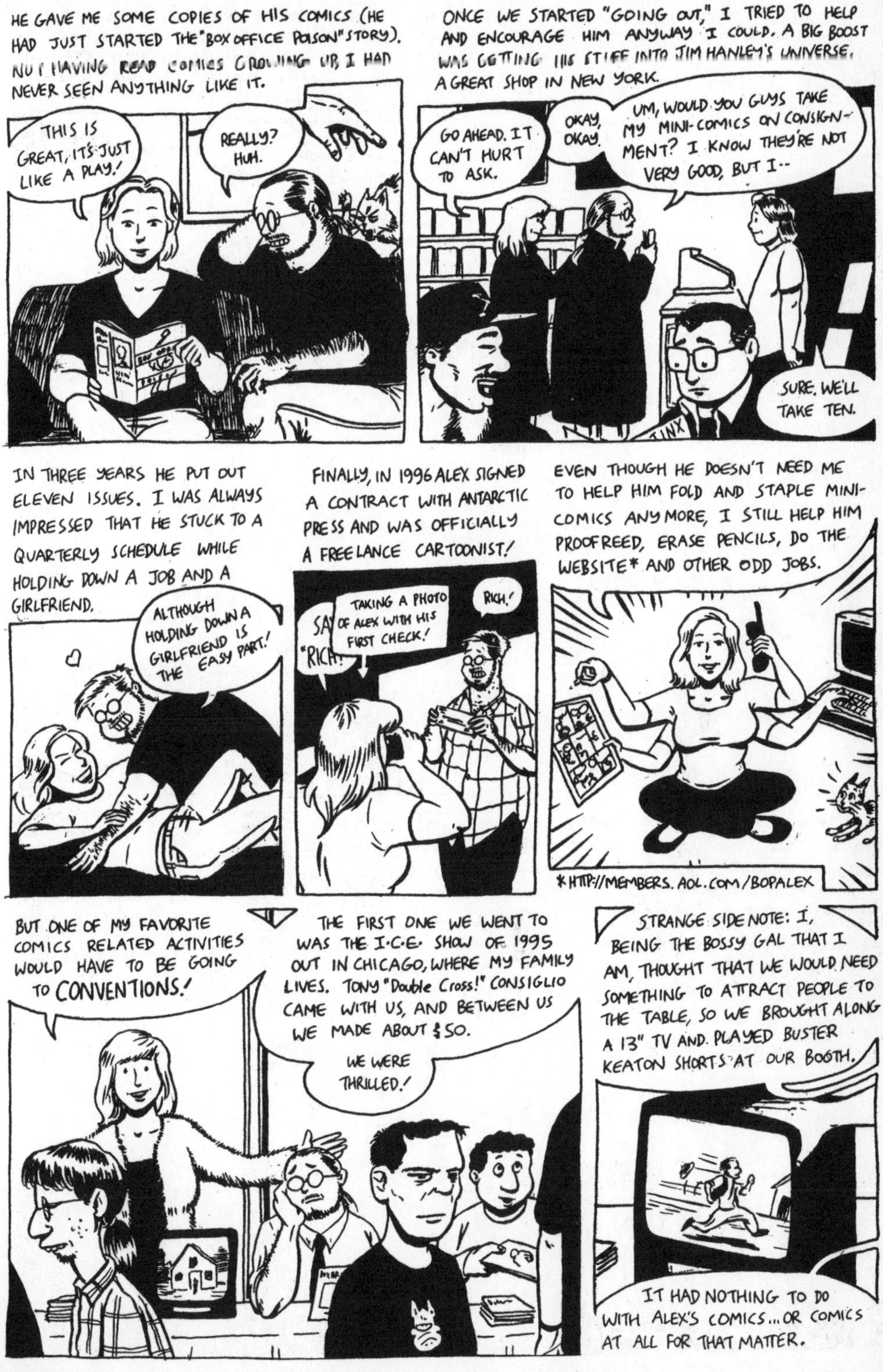
HE GAVE ME SOME COPIES OF HIS COMICS (HE HAD JUST STARTED THE "BOX OFFICE POISON" STORY). NOT HAVING READ COMICS GROWING UP, I HAD NEVER SEEN ANYTHING LIKE IT.
THIS IS GREAT, IT'S JUST LIKE A PLAY!
REALLY? HUH.
ONCE WE STARTED "GOING OUT," I TRIED TO HELP AND ENCOURAGE HIM ANYWAY I COULD. A BIG BOOST WAS GETTING HIS STUFF INTO JIM HANLEY'S UNIVERSE, A GREAT SHOP IN NEW YORK.
GO AHEAD. IT CAN'T HURT TO ASK.
OKAY, OKAY.
UM, WOULD YOU GUYS TAKE MY MINI-COMICS ON CONSIGNMENT? I KNOW THEY'RE NOT VERY GOOD, BUT I--
SURE. WE'LL TAKE TEN.
JINX
IN THREE YEARS HE PUT OUT ELEVEN ISSUES. I WAS ALWAYS IMPRESSED THAT HE STUCK TO A QUARTERLY SCHEDULE WHILE HOLDING DOWN A JOB AND A GIRLFRIEND.
ALTHOUGH HOLDING DOWN A GIRLFRIEND IS THE EASY PART!
FINALLY, IN 1996 ALEX SIGNED A CONTRACT WITH ANTARCTIC PRESS AND WAS OFFICIALLY A FREELANCE CARTOONIST!
SAY "RICH!"
TAKING A PHOTO OF ALEX WITH HIS FIRST CHECK!
RICH!
EVEN THOUGH HE DOESN'T NEED ME TO HELP HIM FOLD AND STAPLE MINI-COMICS ANYMORE, I STILL HELP HIM PROOFREED, ERASE PENCILS, DO THE WEBSITE* AND OTHER ODD JOBS.
*HTTP://MEMBERS.AOL.COM/BOPALEX
BUT ONE OF MY FAVORITE COMICS RELATED ACTIVITIES WOULD HAVE TO BE GOING TO CONVENTIONS!
THE FIRST ONE WE WENT TO WAS THE I·C·E· SHOW OF 1995 OUT IN CHICAGO, WHERE MY FAMILY LIVES. TONY "Double Cross!" CONSIGLIO CAME WITH US, AND BETWEEN US WE MADE ABOUT $50.
WE WERE THRILLED!
STRANGE SIDE NOTE: I, BEING THE BOSSY GAL THAT I AM, THOUGHT THAT WE WOULD NEED SOMETHING TO ATTRACT PEOPLE TO THE TABLE, SO WE BROUGHT ALONG A 13" TV AND PLAYED BUSTER KEATON SHORTS AT OUR BOOTH.
IT HAD NOTHING TO DO WITH ALEX'S COMICS...OR COMICS AT ALL FOR THAT MATTER.

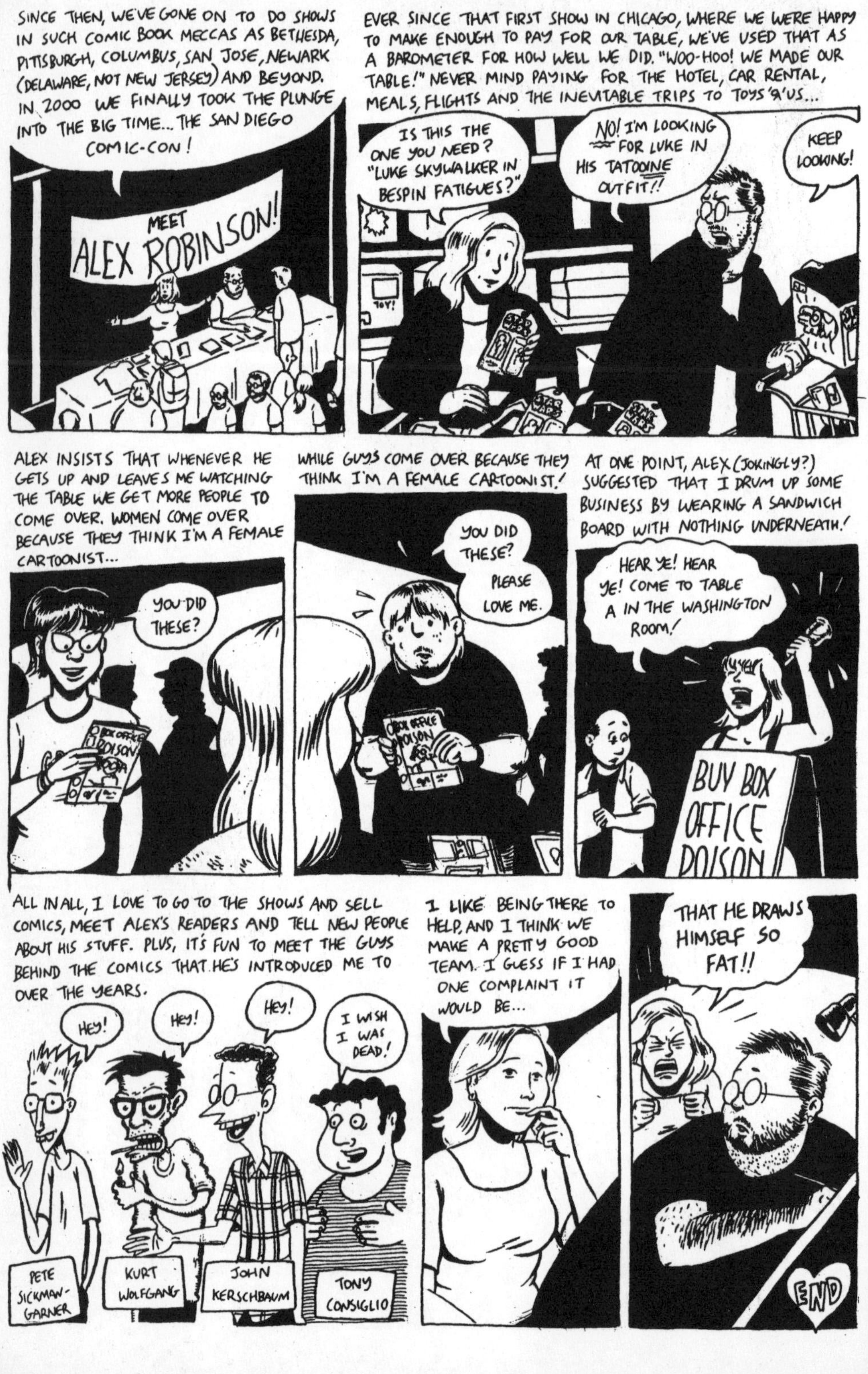
SINCE THEN, WE'VE GONE ON TO DO SHOWS IN SUCH COMIC BOOK MECCAS AS BETHESDA, PITTSBURGH, COLUMBUS, SAN JOSE, NEWARK (DELAWARE, NOT NEW JERSEY) AND BEYOND. IN 2000 WE FINALLY TOOK THE PLUNGE INTO THE BIG TIME... THE SAN DIEGO COMIC-CON!
MEET ALEX ROBINSON!
EVER SINCE THAT FIRST SHOW IN CHICAGO, WHERE WE WERE HAPPY TO MAKE ENOUGH TO PAY FOR OUR TABLE, WE'VE USED THAT AS A BAROMETER FOR HOW WELL WE DID. "WOO-HOO! WE MADE OUR TABLE!" NEVER MIND PAYING FOR THE HOTEL, CAR RENTAL, MEALS, FLIGHTS AND THE INEVITABLE TRIPS TO TOYS 'Я' US...
IS THIS THE ONE YOU NEED? "LUKE SKYWALKER IN BESPIN FATIGUES?"
NO! I'M LOOKING FOR LUKE IN HIS TATOOINE OUTFIT!!
KEEP LOOKING!
TOY!
STAR WARS
ALEX INSISTS THAT WHENEVER HE GETS UP AND LEAVES ME WATCHING THE TABLE WE GET MORE PEOPLE TO COME OVER. WOMEN COME OVER BECAUSE THEY THINK I'M A FEMALE CARTOONIST...
YOU DID THESE?
BOX OFFICE POISON
WHILE GUYS COME OVER BECAUSE THEY THINK I'M A FEMALE CARTOONIST!
YOU DID THESE?
PLEASE LOVE ME.
BOX OFFICE POISON
AT ONE POINT, ALEX (JOKINGLY?) SUGGESTED THAT I DRUM UP SOME BUSINESS BY WEARING A SANDWICH BOARD WITH NOTHING UNDERNEATH!
HEAR YE! HEAR YE! COME TO TABLE A IN THE WASHINGTON ROOM!
BUY BOX OFFICE POISON
ALL IN ALL, I LOVE TO GO TO THE SHOWS AND SELL COMICS, MEET ALEX'S READERS AND TELL NEW PEOPLE ABOUT HIS STUFF. PLUS, IT'S FUN TO MEET THE GUYS BEHIND THE COMICS THAT HE'S INTRODUCED ME TO OVER THE YEARS.
HEY!
HEY!
HEY!
I WISH I WAS DEAD!
PETE SICKMAN-GARNER
KURT WOLFGANG
JOHN KERSCHBAUM
TONY CONSIGLIO
I LIKE BEING THERE TO HELP, AND I THINK WE MAKE A PRETTY GOOD TEAM. I GUESS IF I HAD ONE COMPLAINT IT WOULD BE...
THAT HE DRAWS HIMSELF SO FAT!!
END

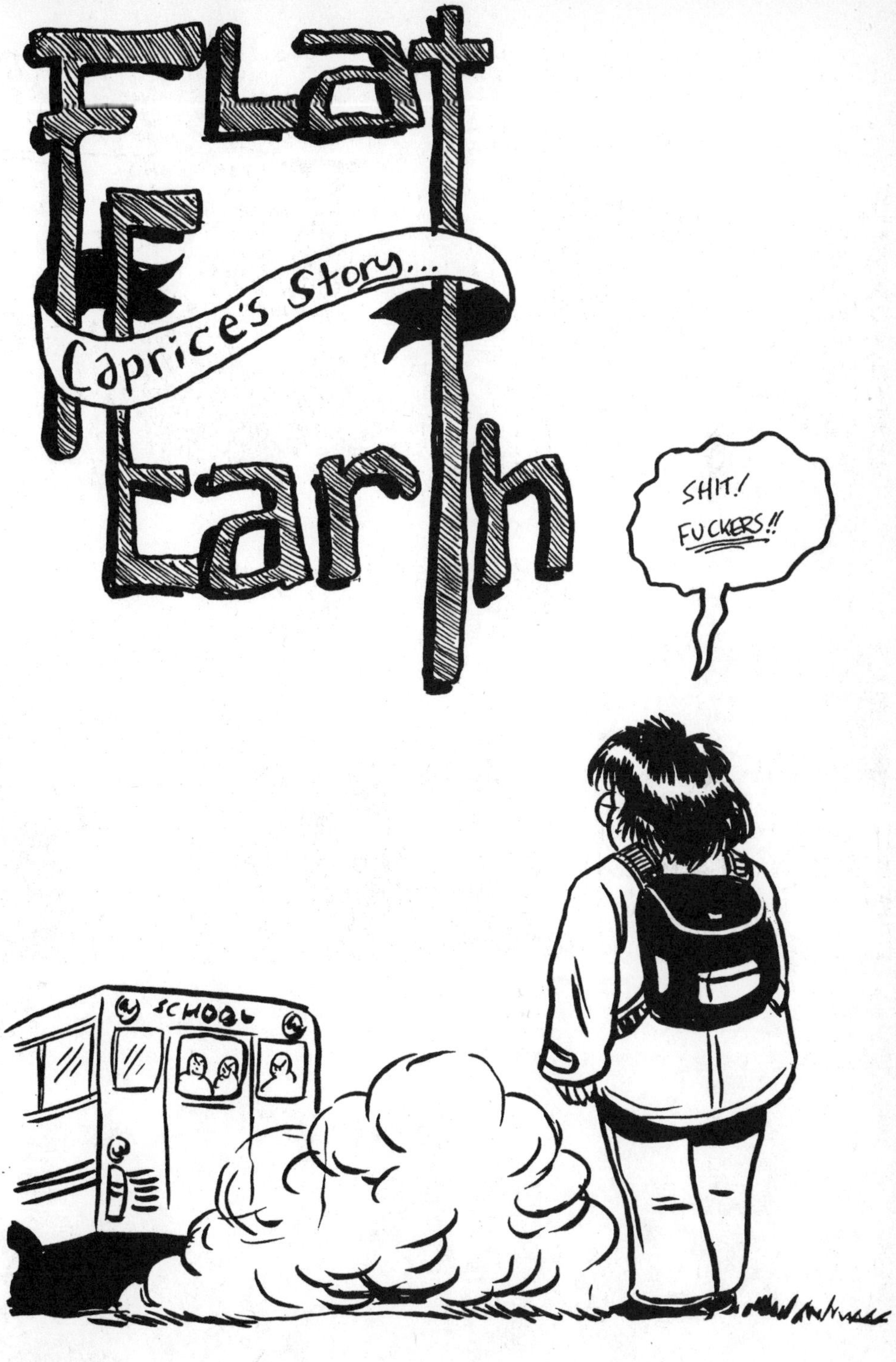
Flat Earth
Caprice's Story...
SHIT! FUCKERS!!
SCHOOL
9:45 AM--TUESDAY, APRIL 2nd!

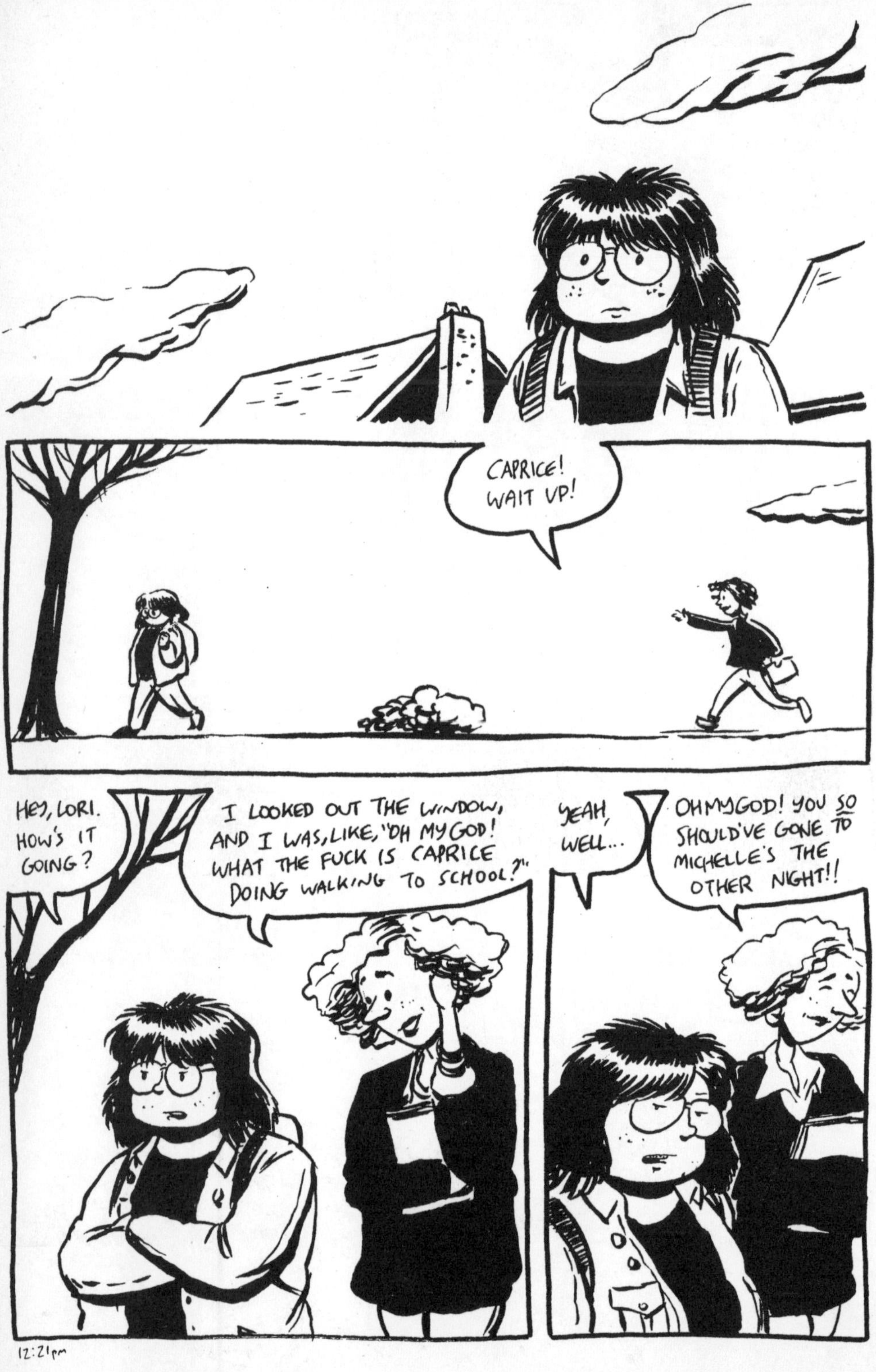
CAPRICE! WAIT UP!
HEY, LORI. HOW'S IT GOING?
I LOOKED OUT THE WINDOW, AND I WAS, LIKE, "OH MY GOD! WHAT THE FUCK IS CAPRICE DOING WALKING TO SCHOOL?"
YEAH, WELL...
OHMYGOD! YOU SO SHOULD'VE GONE TO MICHELLE'S THE OTHER NIGHT!!
12:21pm

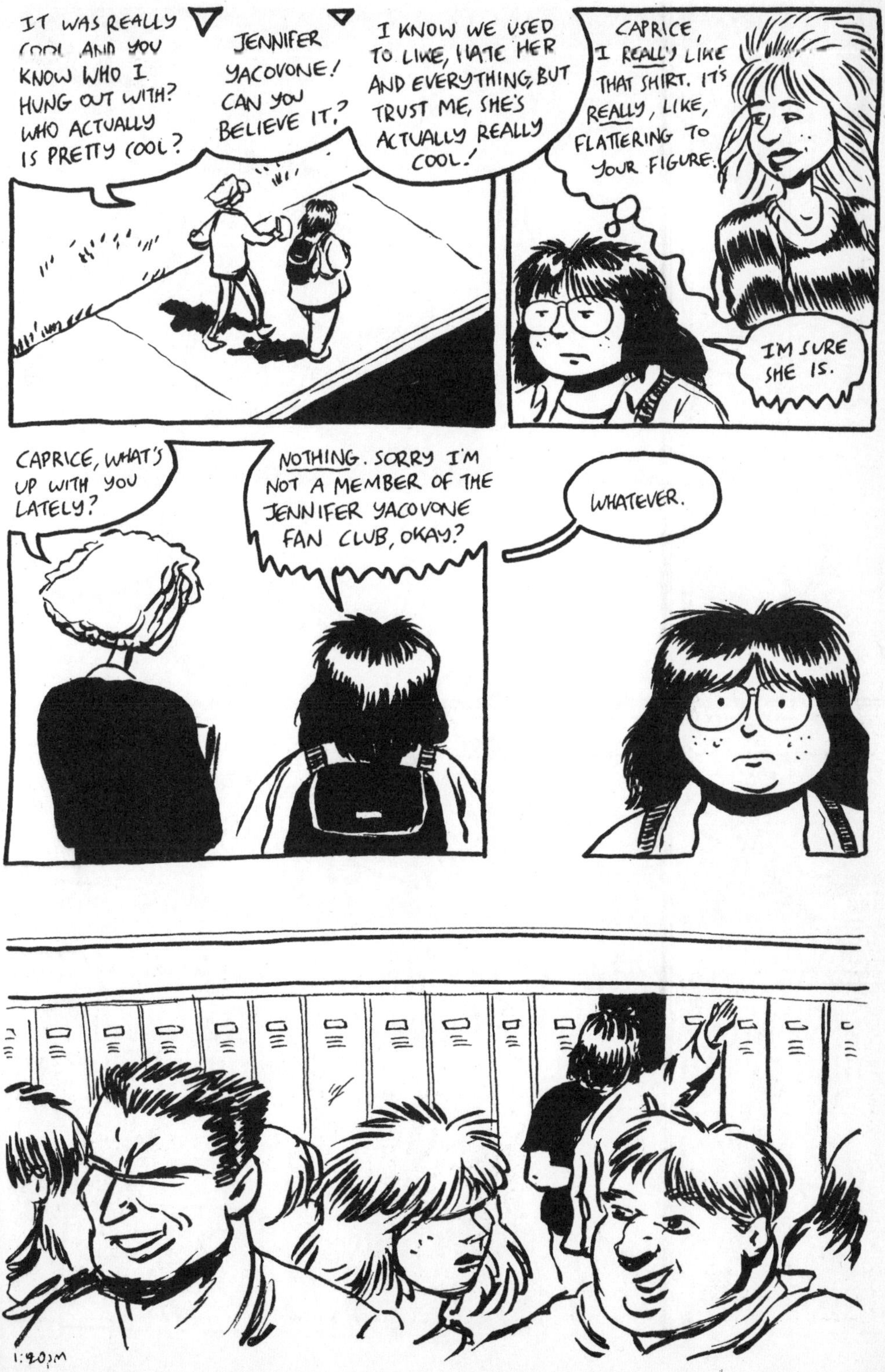
IT WAS REALLY COOL AND YOU KNOW WHO I HUNG OUT WITH? WHO ACTUALLY IS PRETTY COOL?
JENNIFER YACOVONE! CAN YOU BELIEVE IT?
I KNOW WE USED TO LIKE, HATE HER AND EVERYTHING, BUT TRUST ME, SHE'S ACTUALLY REALLY COOL!
CAPRICE, I REALLY LIKE THAT SHIRT. IT'S REALLY, LIKE, FLATTERING TO YOUR FIGURE.
I'M SURE SHE IS.
CAPRICE, WHAT'S UP WITH YOU LATELY?
NOTHING. SORRY I'M NOT A MEMBER OF THE JENNIFER YACOVONE FAN CLUB, OKAY?
WHATEVER.
1:20pm

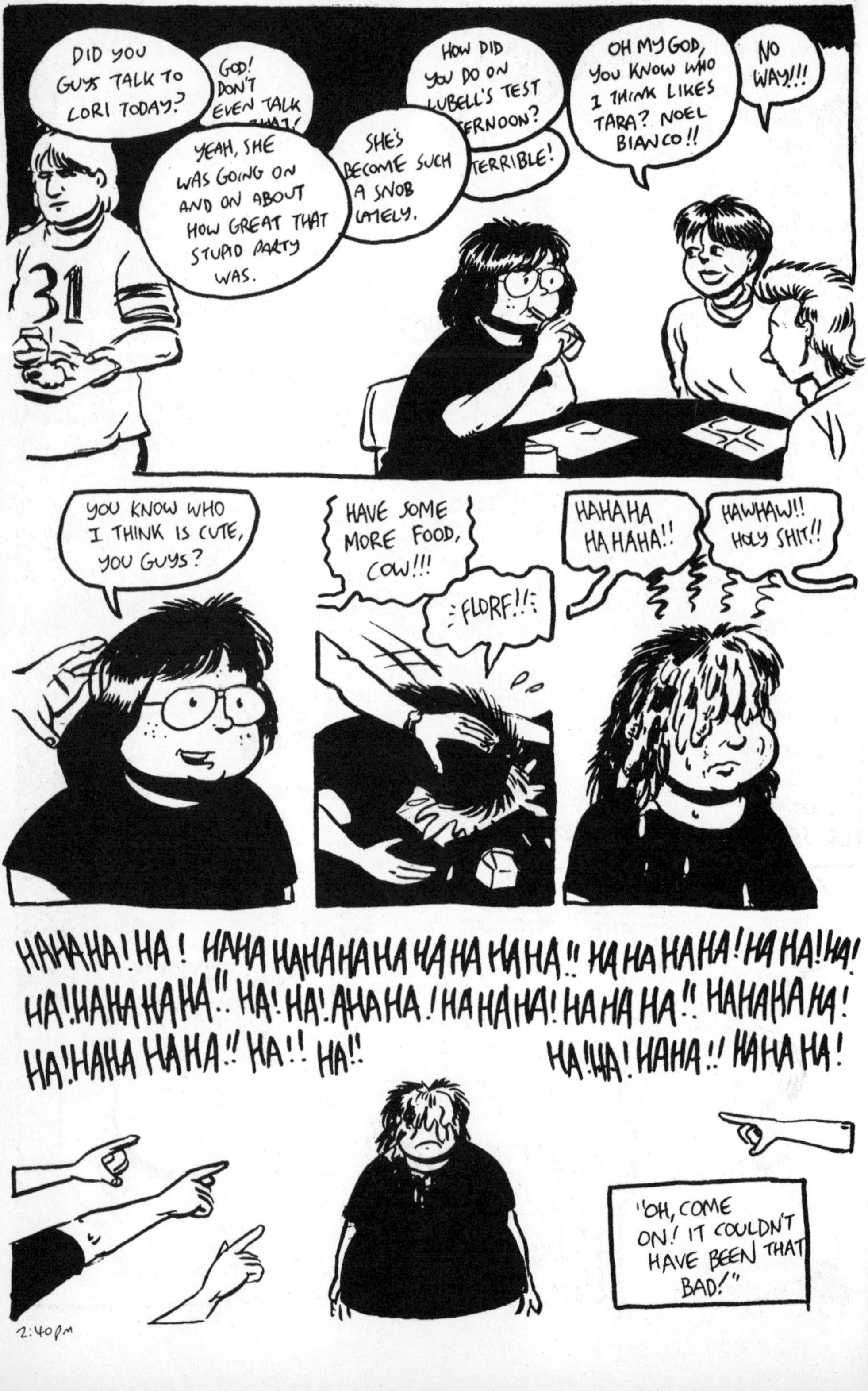

DID YOU GUYS TALK TO LORI TODAY?
GOD! DON'T EVEN TALK
YEAH, SHE WAS GOING ON AND ON ABOUT HOW GREAT THAT STUPID PARTY WAS.
SHE'S BECOME SUCH A SNOB LATELY.
HOW DID YOU DO ON LUBELL'S TEST
TERRIBLE!
OH MY GOD, YOU KNOW WHO I THINK LIKES TARA? NOEL BIANCO!!
NO WAY!!!
YOU KNOW WHO I THINK IS CUTE, YOU GUYS?
HAVE SOME MORE FOOD, COW!!!
FLORF!!
HAHAHA HAHAHA!!
HAWHAW!! HOLY SHIT!!
HAHAHA! HA! HAHA HAHAHAHA HA HA HAHA!! HA HA HAHA! HA HA! HA!
HA! HAHA HAHA!! HA! HA! AHAHA! HA HAHA! HA HA HA!! HAHAHA HA!
HA! HAHA HAHA!! HA!! HA!! HA! HA! HAHA!! HAHA HA!
"OH, COME ON! IT COULDN'T HAVE BEEN THAT BAD!"
2:40pm

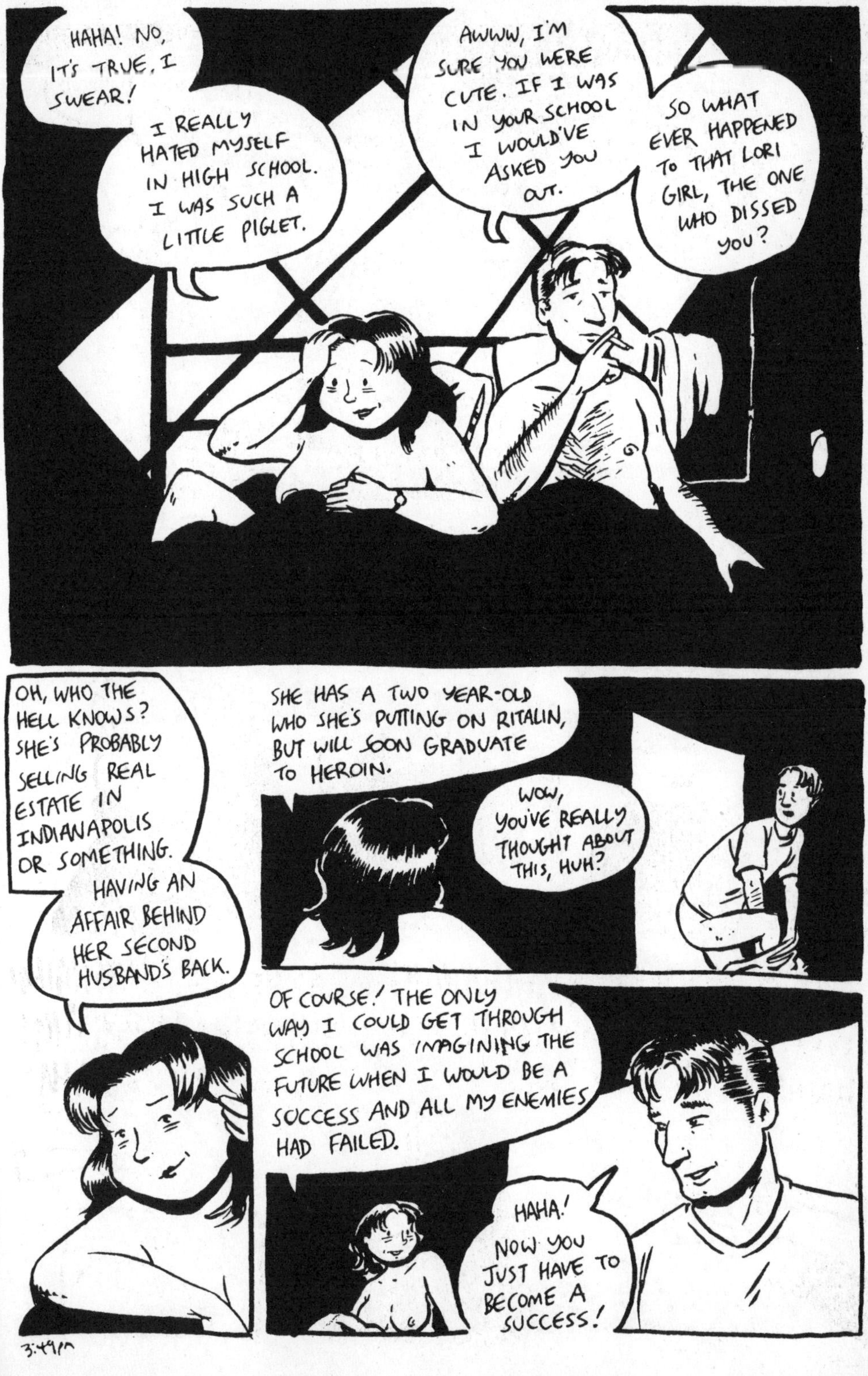
HAHA! NO, IT'S TRUE. I SWEAR!
I REALLY HATED MYSELF IN HIGH SCHOOL. I WAS SUCH A LITTLE PIGLET.
AWWW, I'M SURE YOU WERE CUTE. IF I WAS IN YOUR SCHOOL I WOULD'VE ASKED YOU OUT.
SO WHAT EVER HAPPENED TO THAT LORI GIRL, THE ONE WHO DISSED YOU?
OH, WHO THE HELL KNOWS? SHE'S PROBABLY SELLING REAL ESTATE IN INDIANAPOLIS OR SOMETHING.
SHE HAS A TWO YEAR-OLD WHO SHE'S PUTTING ON RITALIN, BUT WILL SOON GRADUATE TO HEROIN.
WOW, YOU'VE REALLY THOUGHT ABOUT THIS, HUH?
HAVING AN AFFAIR BEHIND HER SECOND HUSBAND'S BACK.
OF COURSE! THE ONLY WAY I COULD GET THROUGH SCHOOL WAS IMAGINING THE FUTURE WHEN I WOULD BE A SUCCESS AND ALL MY ENEMIES HAD FAILED.
HAHA! NOW YOU JUST HAVE TO BECOME A SUCCESS!

3:49pm

WAIT, WHAT'S THAT SUPPOSED TO MEAN? I'M... I THINK OF MYSELF AS SUCCESSFUL.

I GUESS SO. I JUST MEANT THAT...

I MEAN YOU DON'T HAVE THE KIND OF SUCCESS PEOPLE HAVE WHEN THEY THINK OF SHOWING UP PEOPLE, YOU KNOW?

THANKS ALOT, KEVIN!

NO, COME ON. I'M NOT TRYING TO BE, LIKE, MEAN OR ANYTHING, BUT LET'S FACE IT: YOU'RE NOT A BRAIN SURGEON, YOU'RE A WAITRESS.

AND YOU COULD STILL STAND TO LOSE A FEW POUNDS.

COME ON, START TO GET READY.

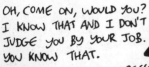

YOU KNOW I'M ONLY WAITING TABLES UNTIL I CAN FIGURE OUT WHAT TO DO.

OH, COME ON, WOULD YOU? I KNOW THAT AND I DON'T JUDGE YOU BY YOUR JOB. YOU KNOW THAT.

NOW, GET DRESSED, PLEASE? WE'RE SUPPOSED TO MEET THEM IN LIKE FIFTEEN MINUTES!

4:48 PM

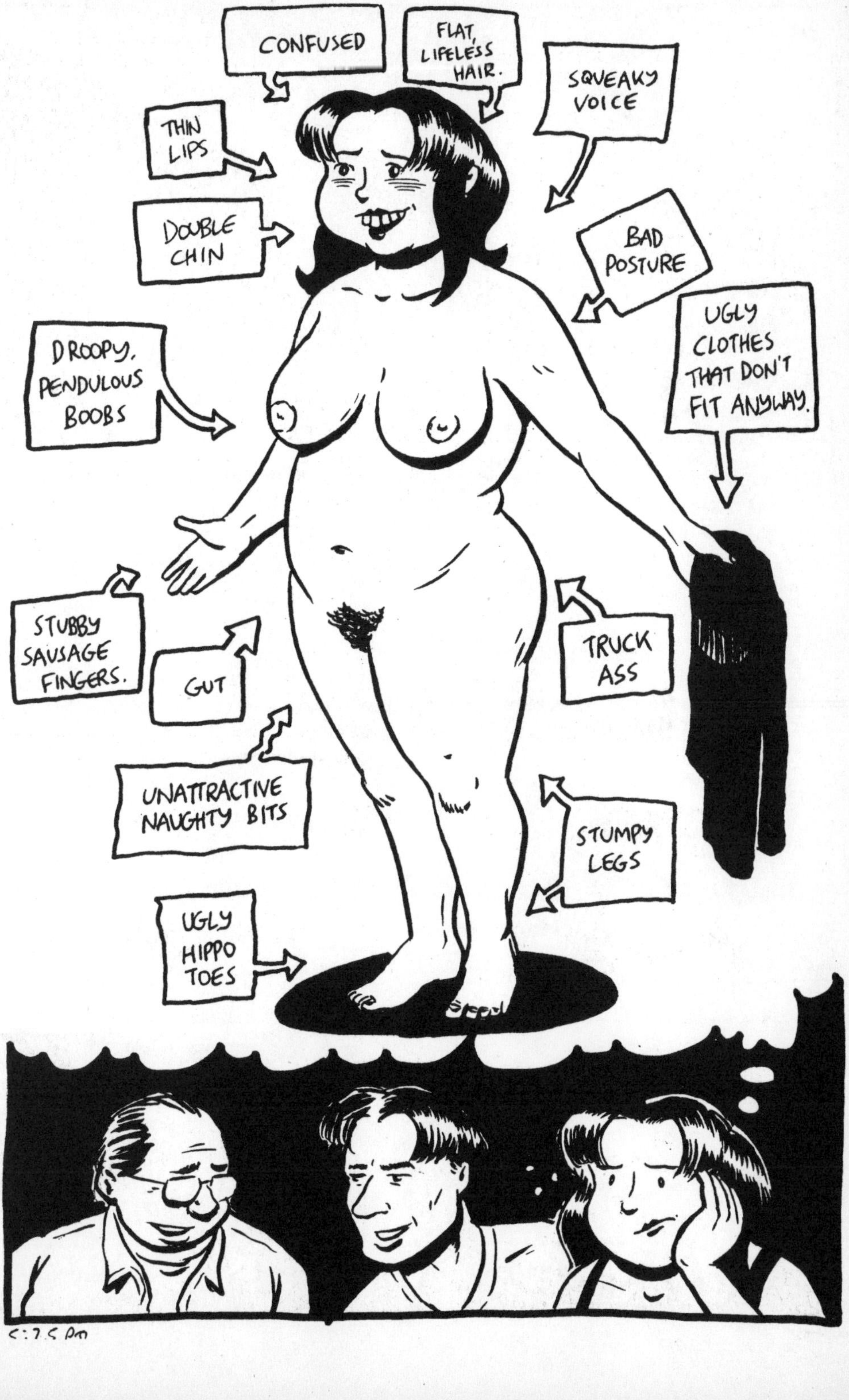
CONFUSED
FLAT, LIFELESS HAIR.
SQUEAKY VOICE
THIN LIPS
DOUBLE CHIN
BAD POSTURE
UGLY CLOTHES THAT DON'T FIT ANYWAY.
DROOPY, PENDULOUS BOOBS
STUBBY SAUSAGE FINGERS.
GUT
TRUCK ASS
UNATTRACTIVE NAUGHTY BITS
STUMPY LEGS
UGLY HIPPO TOES

♪ I know what it is to be sad...and she's making me feel like...

HEY. WHAT'RE YOU DOING?

MMM!

HEY, KAREN! WELCOME HOME! I WAS JUST NOODLING AROUND ON THE WEB.

▽ HOW WAS HOUSTON?

GOD, IT WAS AWFUL! YOU'D THINK A CONVENTION OF SPACE NERDS WOULD AT LEAST BE, Y'KNOW, INTERESTING, BUT IT SUCKED.

HOW WERE THE KITTIES?

OH, THEY WERE FINE. STINKY WAS A LITTLE BRAT AS-- AHA!

WHAT... "HIGHSCHOOL CHUMS.COM?"

Hch hch... YEAH. I'M TRYING TO FIND OUT WHAT HAPPENED TO THIS GIRL I ONCE KNEW, AND HERE SHE IS!

highschoolchums

CLASS OF 198
LORI CLINCHY

6:29 PM

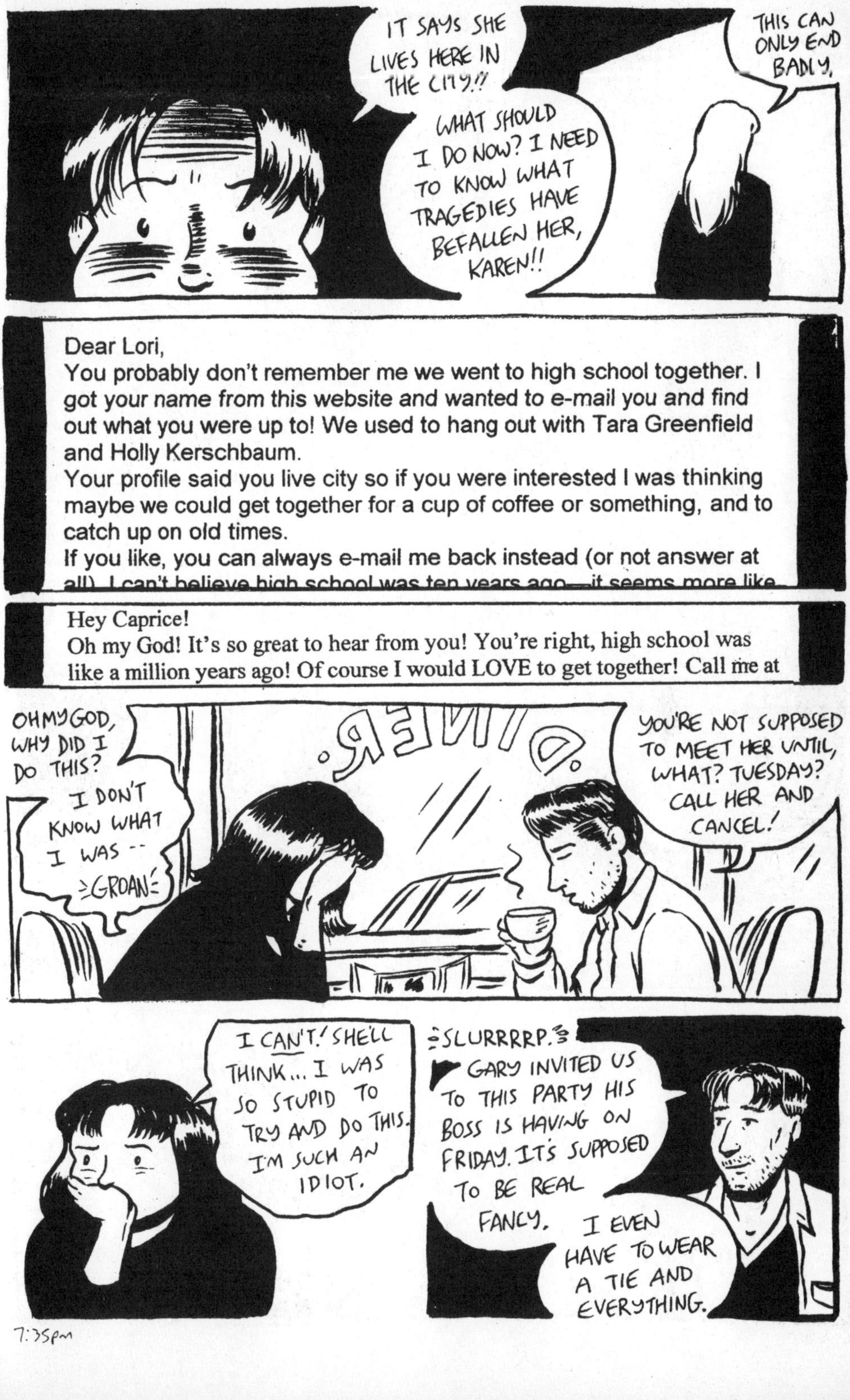
IT SAYS SHE LIVES HERE IN THE CITY!!
WHAT SHOULD I DO NOW? I NEED TO KNOW WHAT TRAGEDIES HAVE BEFALLEN HER, KAREN!!
THIS CAN ONLY END BADLY.
Dear Lori,
You probably don't remember me we went to high school together. I got your name from this website and wanted to e-mail you and find out what you were up to! We used to hang out with Tara Greenfield and Holly Kerschbaum.
Your profile said you live city so if you were interested I was thinking maybe we could get together for a cup of coffee or something, and to catch up on old times.
If you like, you can always e-mail me back instead (or not answer at
Hey Caprice!
Oh my God! It's so great to hear from you! You're right, high school was like a million years ago! Of course I would LOVE to get together! Call me at
OHMYGOD, WHY DID I DO THIS?
I DON'T KNOW WHAT I WAS -- GROAN
DINER
YOU'RE NOT SUPPOSED TO MEET HER UNTIL, WHAT? TUESDAY? CALL HER AND CANCEL!
I CAN'T! SHE'LL THINK... I WAS SO STUPID TO TRY AND DO THIS. I'M SUCH AN IDIOT.
SLURRRRP.
GARY INVITED US TO THIS PARTY HIS BOSS IS HAVING ON FRIDAY. IT'S SUPPOSED TO BE REAL FANCY.
I EVEN HAVE TO WEAR A TIE AND EVERYTHING.

7:35pm

I GUESS I JUST HAVE TO GO THROUGH WITH IT. I GUESS IT'LL TEACH ME A LESSON.
SO MAKE SURE YOU WEAR SOMETHING NICE, OKAY?
OF COURSE! I DON'T WANT HER TO THINK I'M SOME SLOB!
CAN'T TAKE MY
THEY HAD TO TAKE OFF MY THUMBS!
MY HUSBAND IS A WOMAN NOW!
LIFE
AWFUL
CAPRICE? CAPRICE SANBERG? OH MY GOD!!
OH MY GOD, LORI CLINCH, HOW ARE YOU?
HAHA! WELL FIRST OF ALL I'M LORI THOMPSON NOW! I'VE BEEN MARRIED FOR TWO YEARS!
YOU LOOK GREAT!

8:50pm

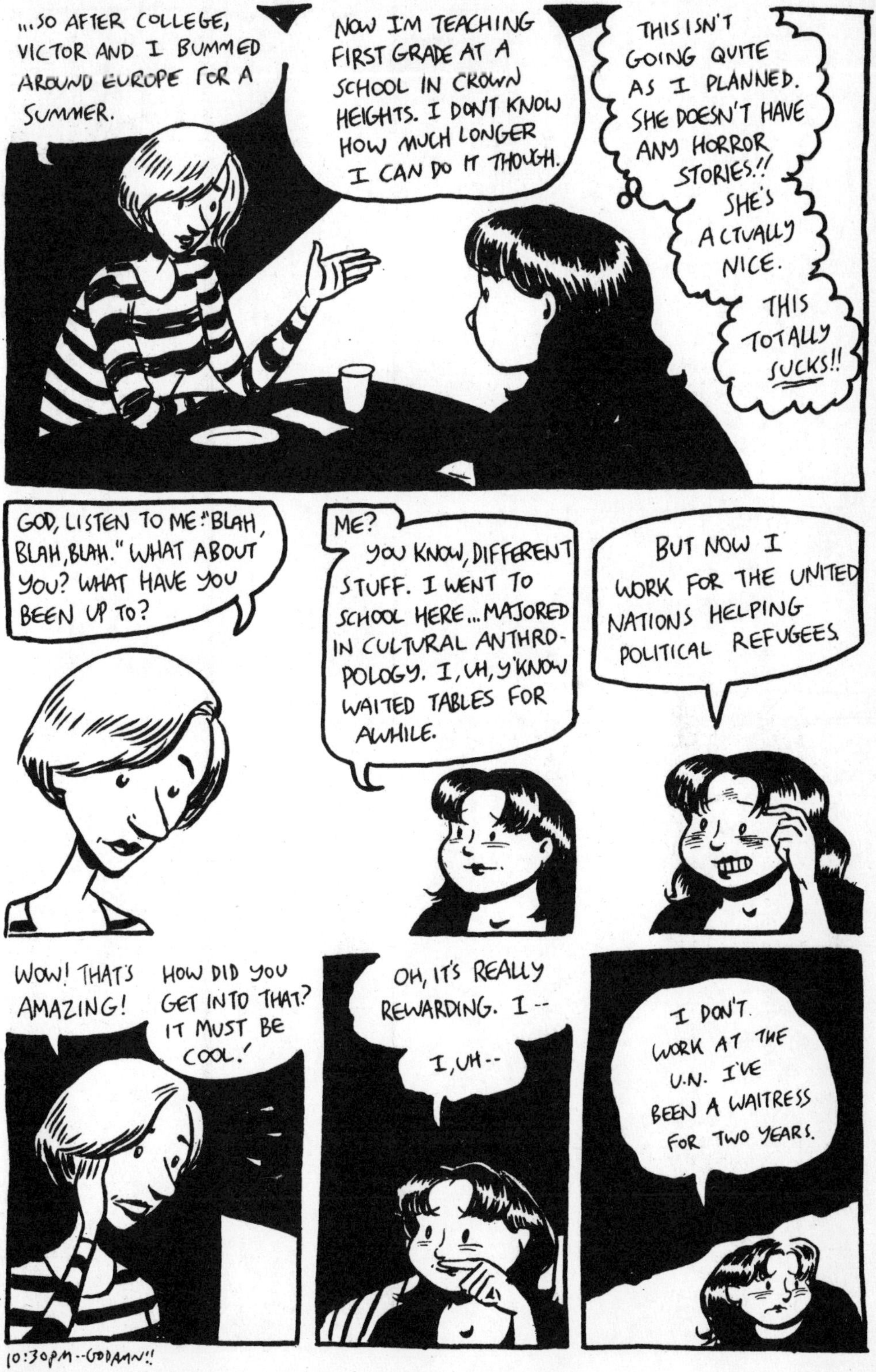
...SO AFTER COLLEGE, VICTOR AND I BUMMED AROUND EUROPE FOR A SUMMER.
NOW I'M TEACHING FIRST GRADE AT A SCHOOL IN CROWN HEIGHTS. I DON'T KNOW HOW MUCH LONGER I CAN DO IT THOUGH.
THIS ISN'T GOING QUITE AS I PLANNED. SHE DOESN'T HAVE ANY HORROR STORIES!! SHE'S ACTUALLY NICE.
THIS TOTALLY SUCKS!!
GOD, LISTEN TO ME: "BLAH, BLAH, BLAH." WHAT ABOUT YOU? WHAT HAVE YOU BEEN UP TO?
ME? YOU KNOW, DIFFERENT STUFF. I WENT TO SCHOOL HERE... MAJORED IN CULTURAL ANTHROPOLOGY. I, UH, Y'KNOW WAITED TABLES FOR AWHILE.
BUT NOW I WORK FOR THE UNITED NATIONS HELPING POLITICAL REFUGEES.
WOW! THAT'S AMAZING!
HOW DID YOU GET INTO THAT? IT MUST BE COOL!
OH, IT'S REALLY REWARDING. I --
I, UH --
I DON'T WORK AT THE U.N. I'VE BEEN A WAITRESS FOR TWO YEARS.
10:30PM--GODAMN!!

OH, WELL... THAT'S OKAY, YOU KNOW?

YOU SHOULDN'T BE EMBARRASSED ABOUT THAT.

NO, I GUESS NOT. IT'S AN HONEST LIVING, RIGHT?

IT'S JUST THAT WHEN SOMEONE ASKS YOU ABOUT YOUR LIFE AND YOU HAVE TO SUM IT UP, I JUST SOUND LIKE I HAVEN'T DONE MUCH.

TO MAKE IT WORSE... WELL, I SHOULD PROBABLY NOT TELL YOU THIS, BUT, UH, PART OF THE REASON I WANTED TO MEET WAS THAT, UH...

I WANTED TO FIND OUT WHAT, Y'KNOW, UH, BAD THINGS MIGHT'VE HAPPENED TO

...UH...

YOU.

SO NOW I MEET YOU AND YOU ACTUALLY SEEM REAL NICE, SO I FEEL EVEN WORSE. NOT ONLY AM I A TOTAL LOSER, BUT I'M A PETTY, JEALOUS, LIKE, AWFUL PERSON.

DID YOU HEAR ABOUT AMY FRANKFORT?

SHE COMMITED SUICIDE!

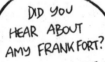

REALLY?

11:39 PM

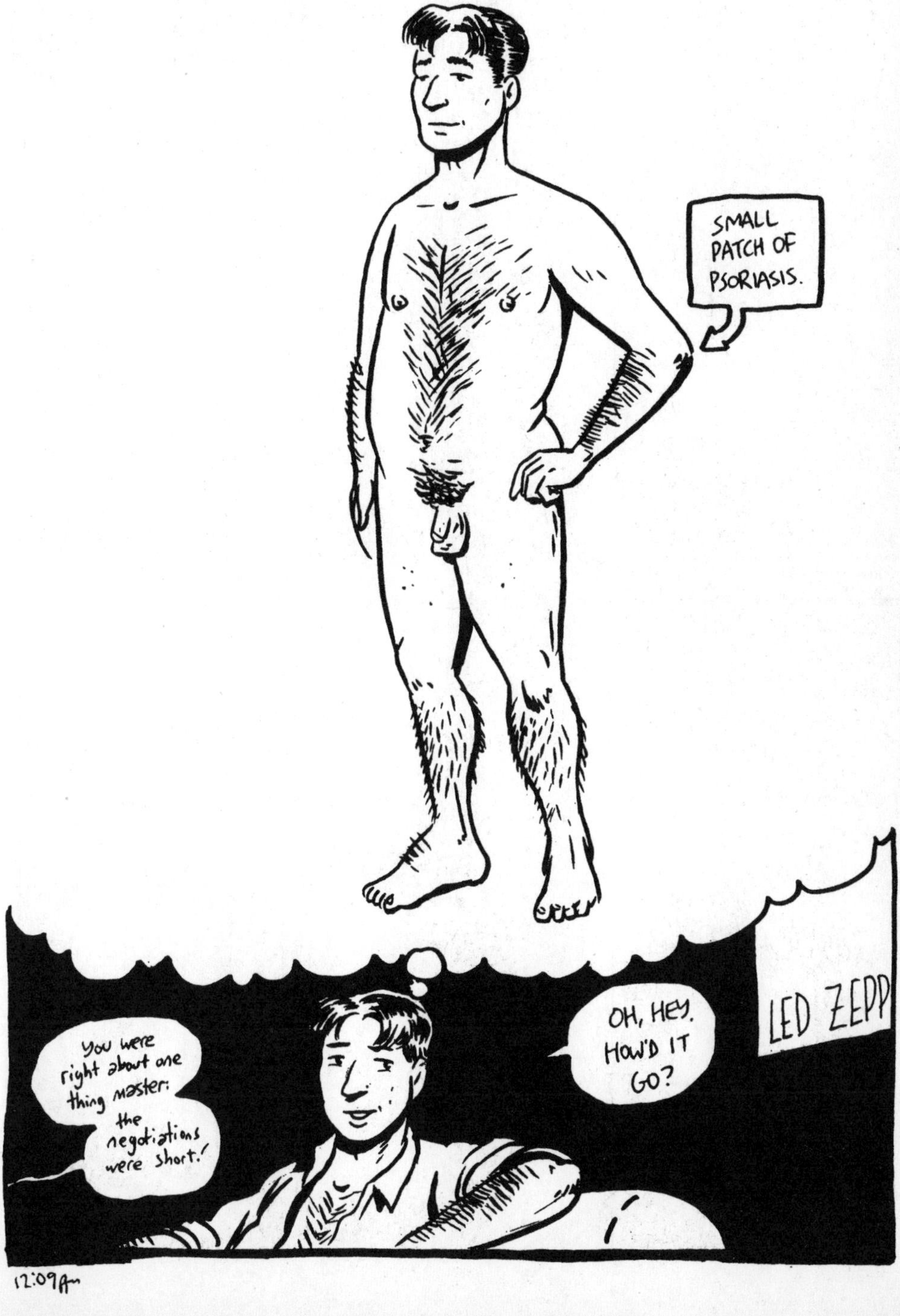
SMALL PATCH OF PSORIASIS.
LED ZEPP
You were right about one thing master: the negotiations were short!
OH, HEY. HOW'D IT GO?

12:09am

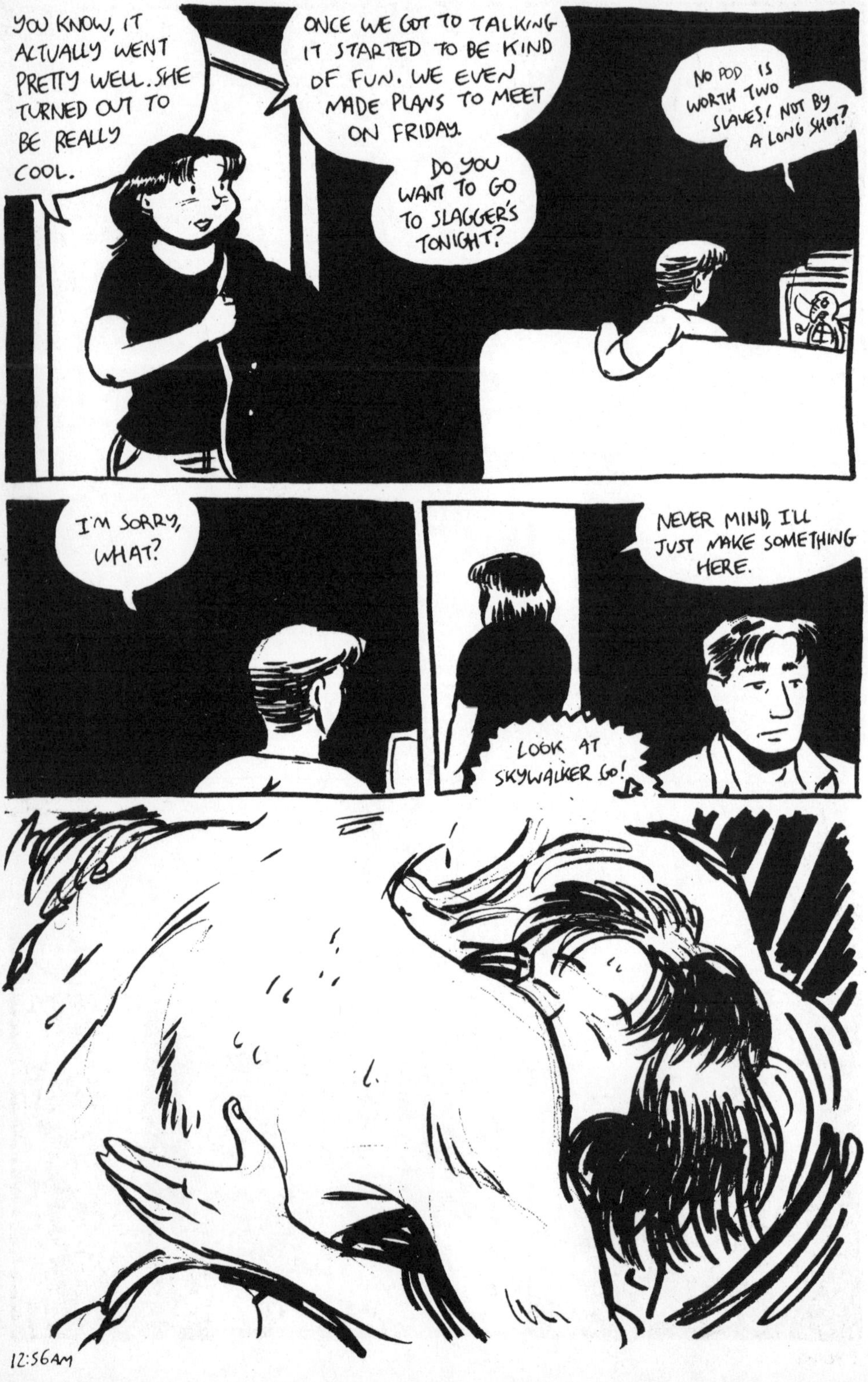
YOU KNOW, IT ACTUALLY WENT PRETTY WELL. SHE TURNED OUT TO BE REALLY COOL.
ONCE WE GOT TO TALKING IT STARTED TO BE KIND OF FUN. WE EVEN MADE PLANS TO MEET ON FRIDAY.
DO YOU WANT TO GO TO SLAGGER'S TONIGHT?
NO POD IS WORTH TWO SLAVES! NOT BY A LONG SHOT!
I'M SORRY, WHAT?
NEVER MIND, I'LL JUST MAKE SOMETHING HERE.
LOOK AT SKYWALKER GO!
12:56AM

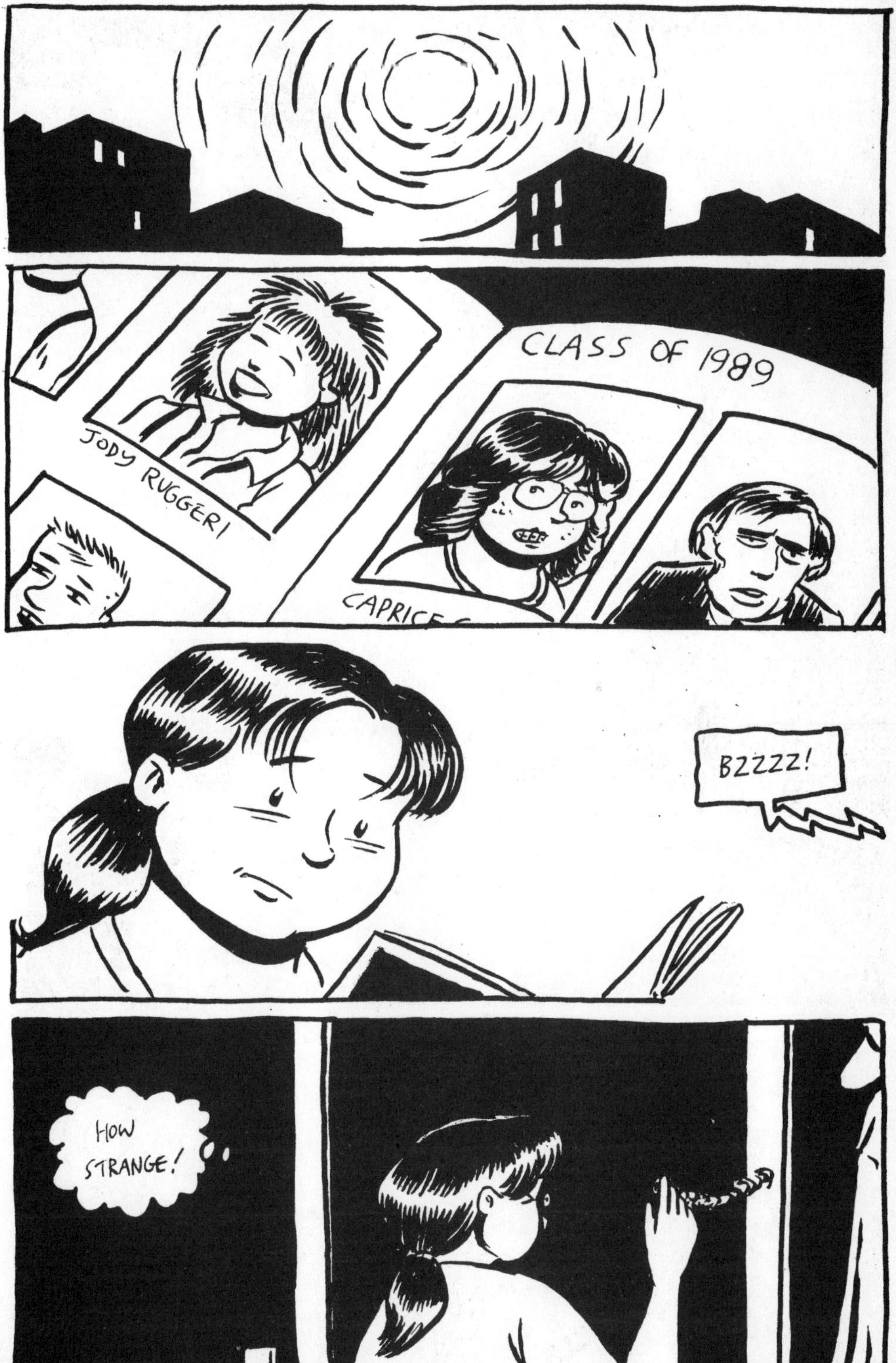
CLASS OF 1989
JODY RUGGERI
CAPRICE
BZZZZ!
HOW STRANGE!
1:46AM

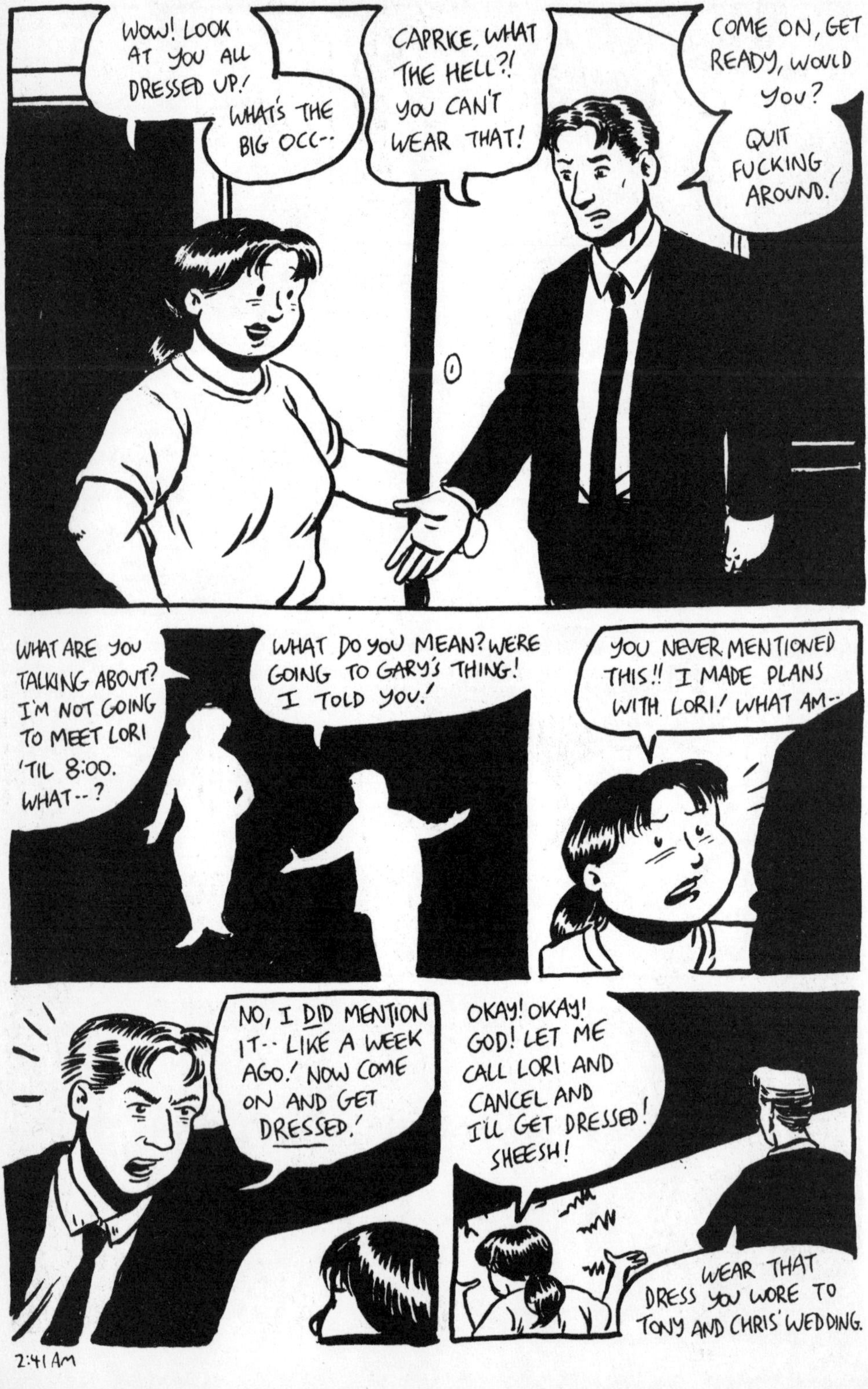
WOW! LOOK AT YOU ALL DRESSED UP!
WHAT'S THE BIG OCC--
CAPRICE, WHAT THE HELL?! YOU CAN'T WEAR THAT!
COME ON, GET READY, WOULD YOU?
QUIT FUCKING AROUND!
WHAT ARE YOU TALKING ABOUT? I'M NOT GOING TO MEET LORI 'TIL 8:00. WHAT--?
WHAT DO YOU MEAN? WE'RE GOING TO GARY'S THING! I TOLD YOU!
YOU NEVER MENTIONED THIS!! I MADE PLANS WITH LORI! WHAT AM--
NO, I DID MENTION IT-- LIKE A WEEK AGO! NOW COME ON AND GET DRESSED!
OKAY! OKAY! GOD! LET ME CALL LORI AND CANCEL AND I'LL GET DRESSED! SHEESH!
WEAR THAT DRESS YOU WORE TO TONY AND CHRIS' WEDDING.

2:41 AM

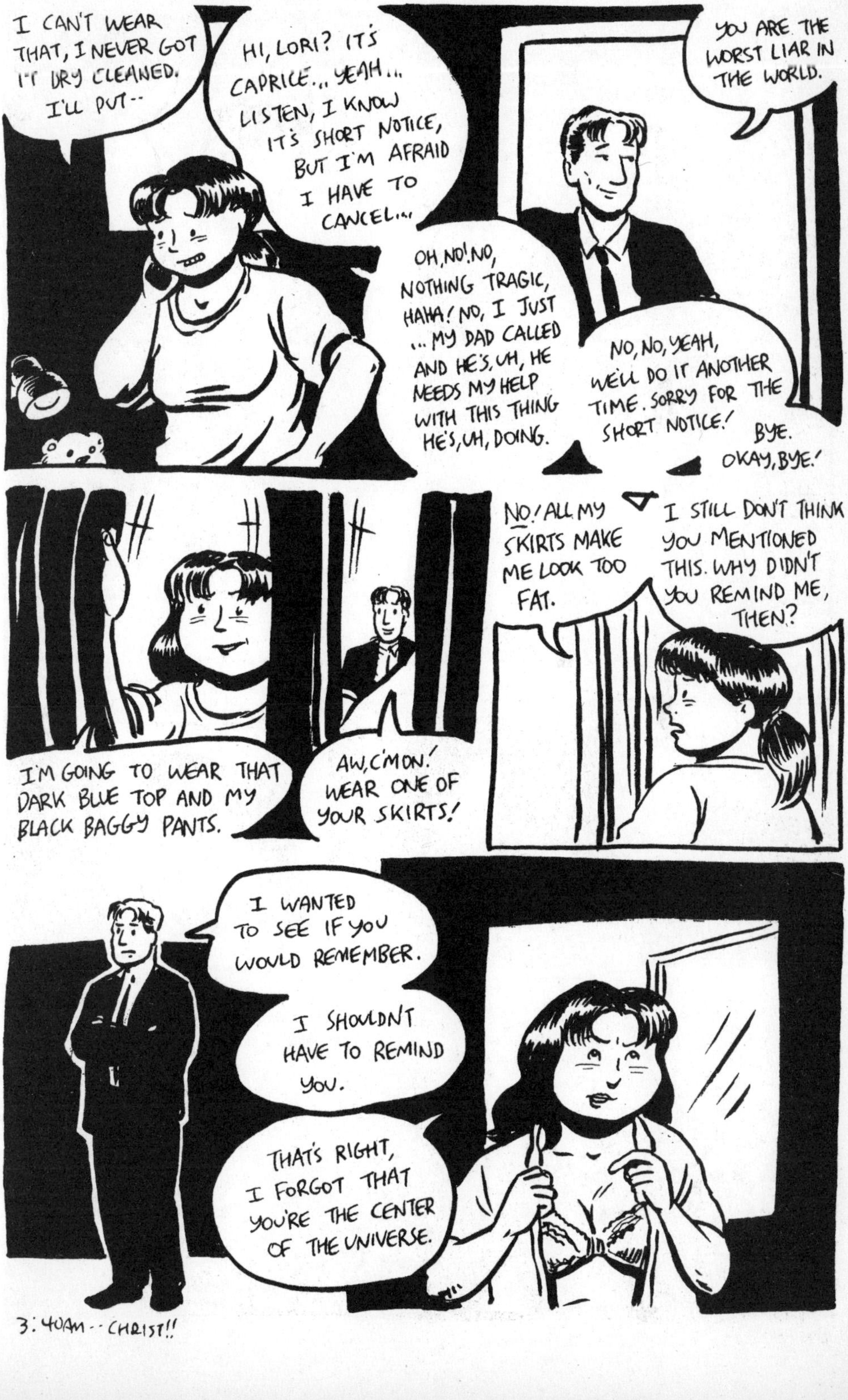
I CAN'T WEAR THAT, I NEVER GOT IT DRY CLEANED. I'LL PUT--
HI, LORI? IT'S CAPRICE... YEAH... LISTEN, I KNOW IT'S SHORT NOTICE, BUT I'M AFRAID I HAVE TO CANCEL...
YOU ARE THE WORST LIAR IN THE WORLD.
OH, NO! NO, NOTHING TRAGIC, HAHA! NO, I JUST ... MY DAD CALLED AND HE'S, UH, HE NEEDS MY HELP WITH THIS THING HE'S, UH, DOING.
NO, NO, YEAH, WE'LL DO IT ANOTHER TIME. SORRY FOR THE SHORT NOTICE!
BYE. OKAY, BYE!
I'M GOING TO WEAR THAT DARK BLUE TOP AND MY BLACK BAGGY PANTS.
AW, C'MON! WEAR ONE OF YOUR SKIRTS!
NO! ALL MY SKIRTS MAKE ME LOOK TOO FAT.
I STILL DON'T THINK YOU MENTIONED THIS. WHY DIDN'T YOU REMIND ME, THEN?
I WANTED TO SEE IF YOU WOULD REMEMBER.
I SHOULDN'T HAVE TO REMIND YOU.
THAT'S RIGHT, I FORGOT THAT YOU'RE THE CENTER OF THE UNIVERSE.
3:40AM -- CHRIST!!

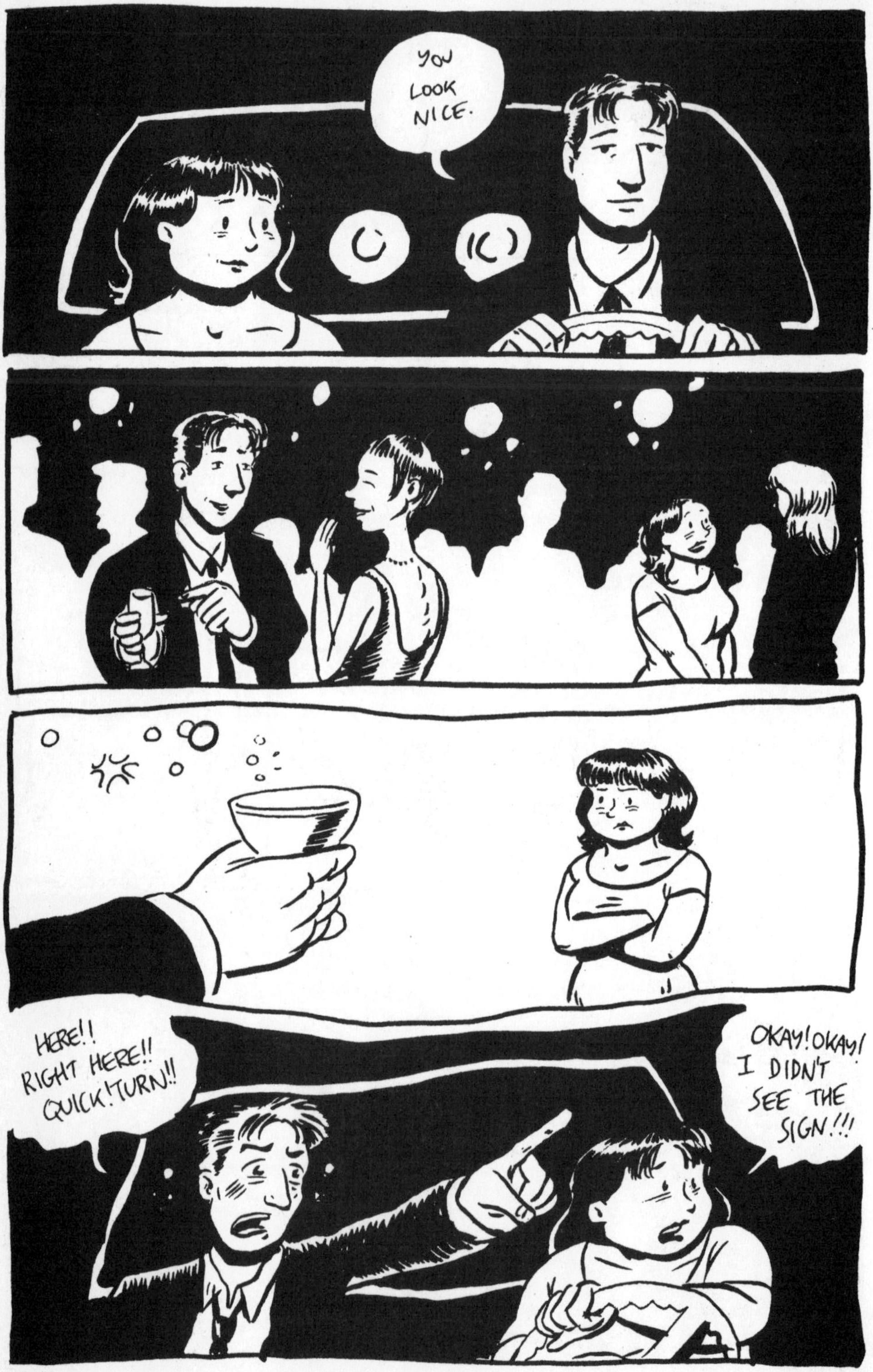
YOU LOOK NICE.
HERE!! RIGHT HERE!! QUICK! TURN!!
OKAY! OKAY! I DIDN'T SEE THE SIGN!!!

5:07AM

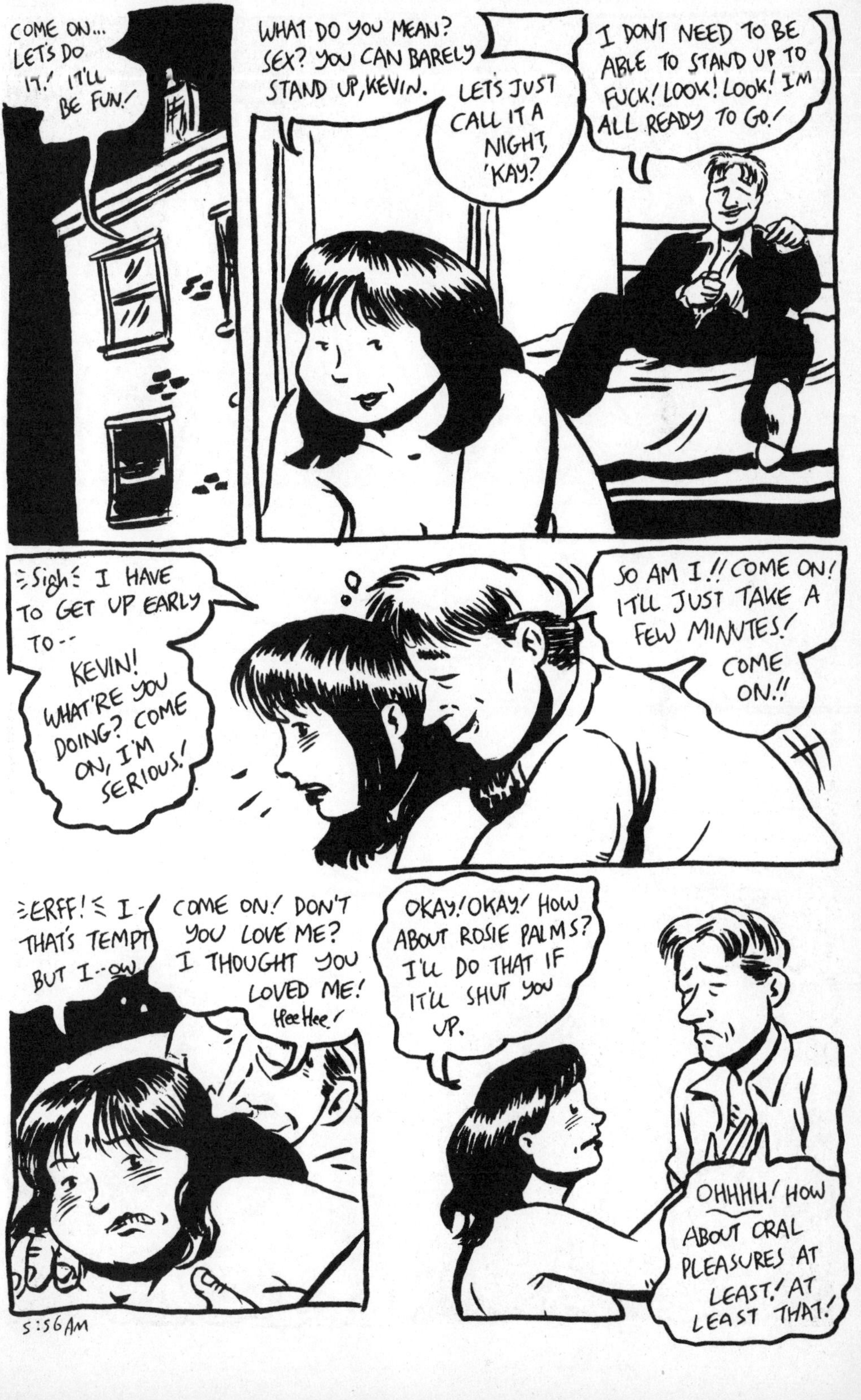
COME ON... LET'S DO IT! IT'LL BE FUN!
WHAT DO YOU MEAN? SEX? YOU CAN BARELY STAND UP, KEVIN.
LET'S JUST CALL IT A NIGHT, 'KAY?
I DON'T NEED TO BE ABLE TO STAND UP TO FUCK! LOOK! LOOK! I'M ALL READY TO GO!
Sigh I HAVE TO GET UP EARLY TO--
SO AM I!! COME ON! IT'LL JUST TAKE A FEW MINUTES!
COME ON!!
KEVIN! WHAT'RE YOU DOING? COME ON, I'M SERIOUS!
ERFF! I- THAT'S TEMPT BUT I--OW
COME ON! DON'T YOU LOVE ME? I THOUGHT YOU LOVED ME!
Hee Hee!
OKAY! OKAY! HOW ABOUT ROSIE PALMS? I'LL DO THAT IF IT'LL SHUT YOU UP.
OHHHH! HOW ABOUT ORAL PLEASURES AT LEAST! AT LEAST THAT!
5:56AM

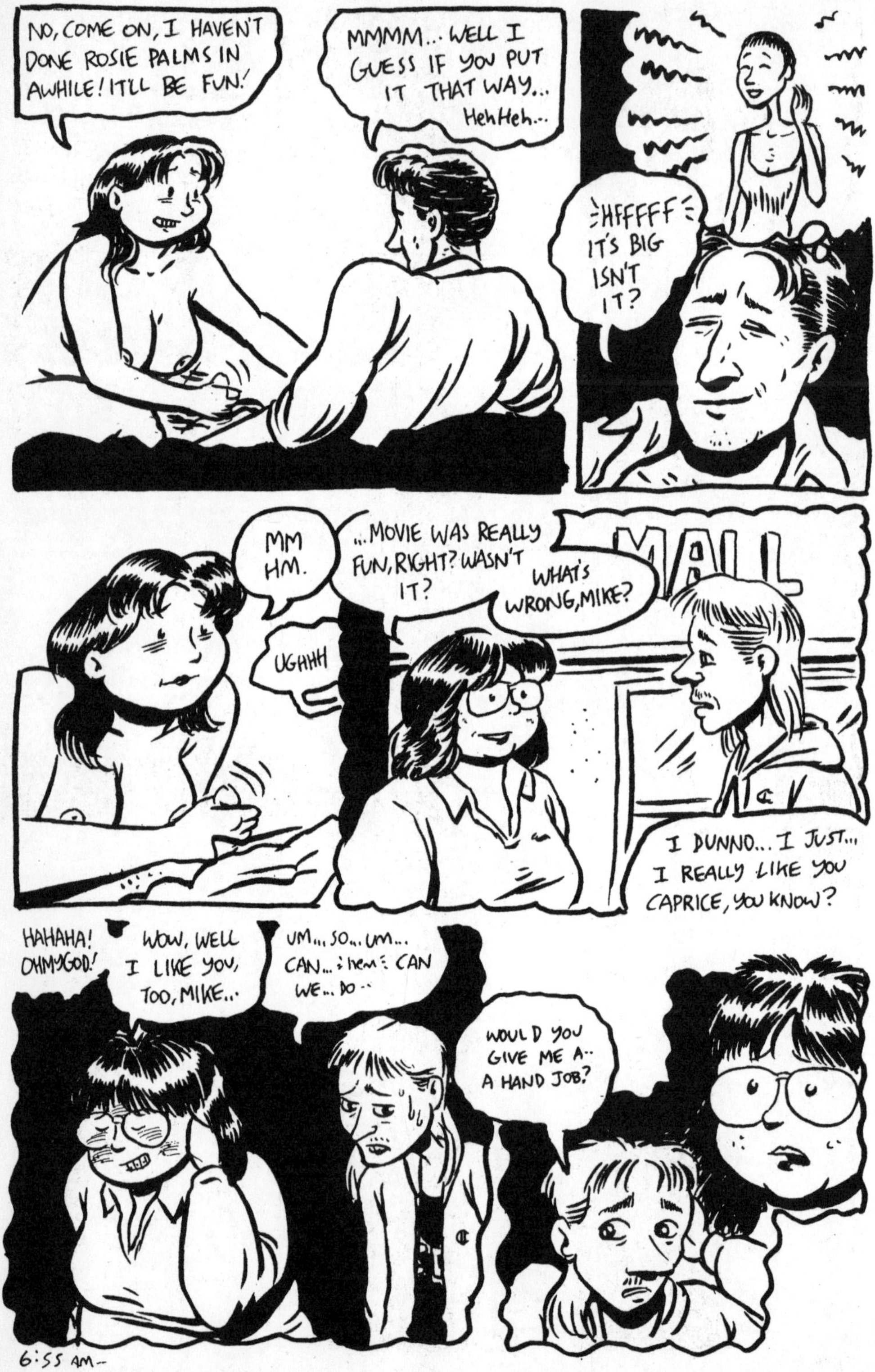

NO, COME ON, I HAVEN'T DONE ROSIE PALMS IN AWHILE! IT'LL BE FUN!
MMMM... WELL I GUESS IF YOU PUT IT THAT WAY... HehHeh...
HFFFFF IT'S BIG ISN'T IT?
MM HM.
...MOVIE WAS REALLY FUN, RIGHT? WASN'T IT?
UGHHH
WHAT'S WRONG, MIKE?
MALL
I DUNNO... I JUST... I REALLY LIKE YOU CAPRICE, YOU KNOW?
HAHAHA! OHMYGOD!
WOW, WELL I LIKE YOU, TOO, MIKE...
UM... SO... UM... CAN... hem CAN WE... DO --
WOULD YOU GIVE ME A.. A HAND JOB?
6:55 AM--

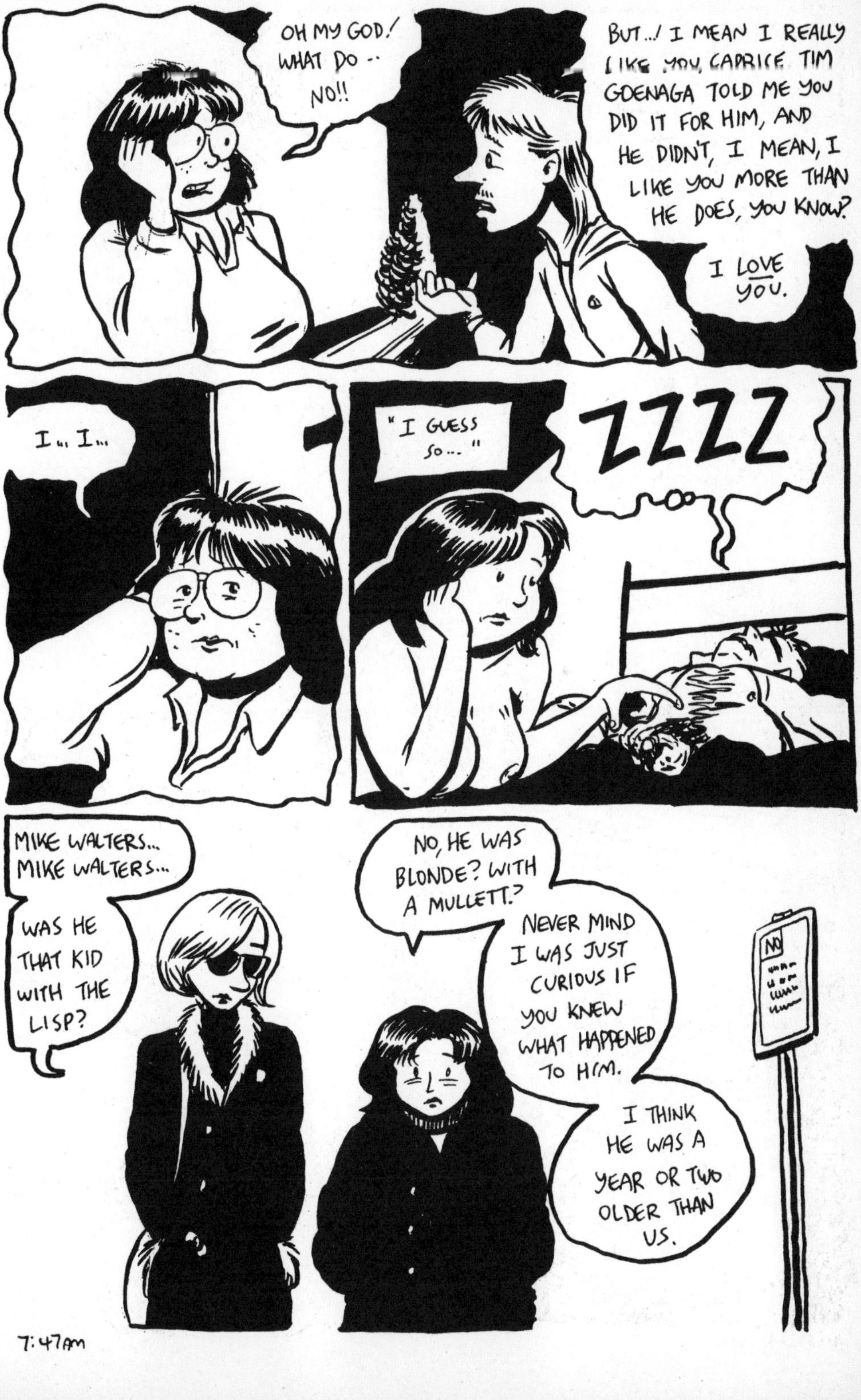
OH MY GOD! WHAT DO -- NO!!
BUT...! I MEAN I REALLY LIKE YOU, CAPRICE. TIM GOENAGA TOLD ME YOU DID IT FOR HIM, AND HE DIDN'T, I MEAN, I LIKE YOU MORE THAN HE DOES, YOU KNOW?
I LOVE YOU.
I... I...
"I GUESS SO..."
ZZZZ
MIKE WALTERS... MIKE WALTERS...
WAS HE THAT KID WITH THE LISP?
NO, HE WAS BLONDE? WITH A MULLETT?
NEVER MIND I WAS JUST CURIOUS IF YOU KNEW WHAT HAPPENED TO HIM.
I THINK HE WAS A YEAR OR TWO OLDER THAN US.
NO
7:47AM

MY BOYFRIEND KEVIN SAYS I'M TOO OBSESSED WITH HIGH SCHOOL.
I PROBABLY THINK ABOUT IT MORE THAN I SHOULD. HE'S RIGHT ABOUT THAT.
DO YOU REMEMBER SCOTT SPURGEON?
I THINK SO. HE WAS, LIKE, ONE OF THE JOCKS, RIGHT?
HE PLAYED SOME SPORTS, YE BUT THE POINT IS THAT I WAS, LIKE, MADLY IN LOVE WITH HIM. LIKE, SERIOUS.
I REALLY HOPED HE WOULD ASK ME OUT, BUT HE NEVER DID. HE MOSTLY WENT FOR Y'KNOW, CHEERLEADER TYPES.
LIKE CINDY SANDERS? GOD, I HATED HER!
YEAH, ME TOO. BUT EVEN THOUGH I'M HAPPY WITH MY LIFE AND ALL, I SOMETIMES WONDER WHAT IT WOULD'VE BEEN LIKE IF SCOTT HAD ASKED ME OUT. IT'S STUPID, RIGHT?
:SIGH: YOU'RE ASKING THE WRONG PERSON, LORI. LIKE I SAID, I SPEND AN UNHEALTHY AMOUNT OF TIME THINKING ABOUT IT.
"SHOULD I HAVE DONE THIS?" "SHOULD I NOT HAVE DONE THIS OTHER THING?"
YOU MAKE YOUR CHOICES AND LIVE WITH THEM I GUESS, RIGHT?
I GUESS THE POINT IS THAT YOU'RE HAPPIER NOW, RIGHT?
8:18AM

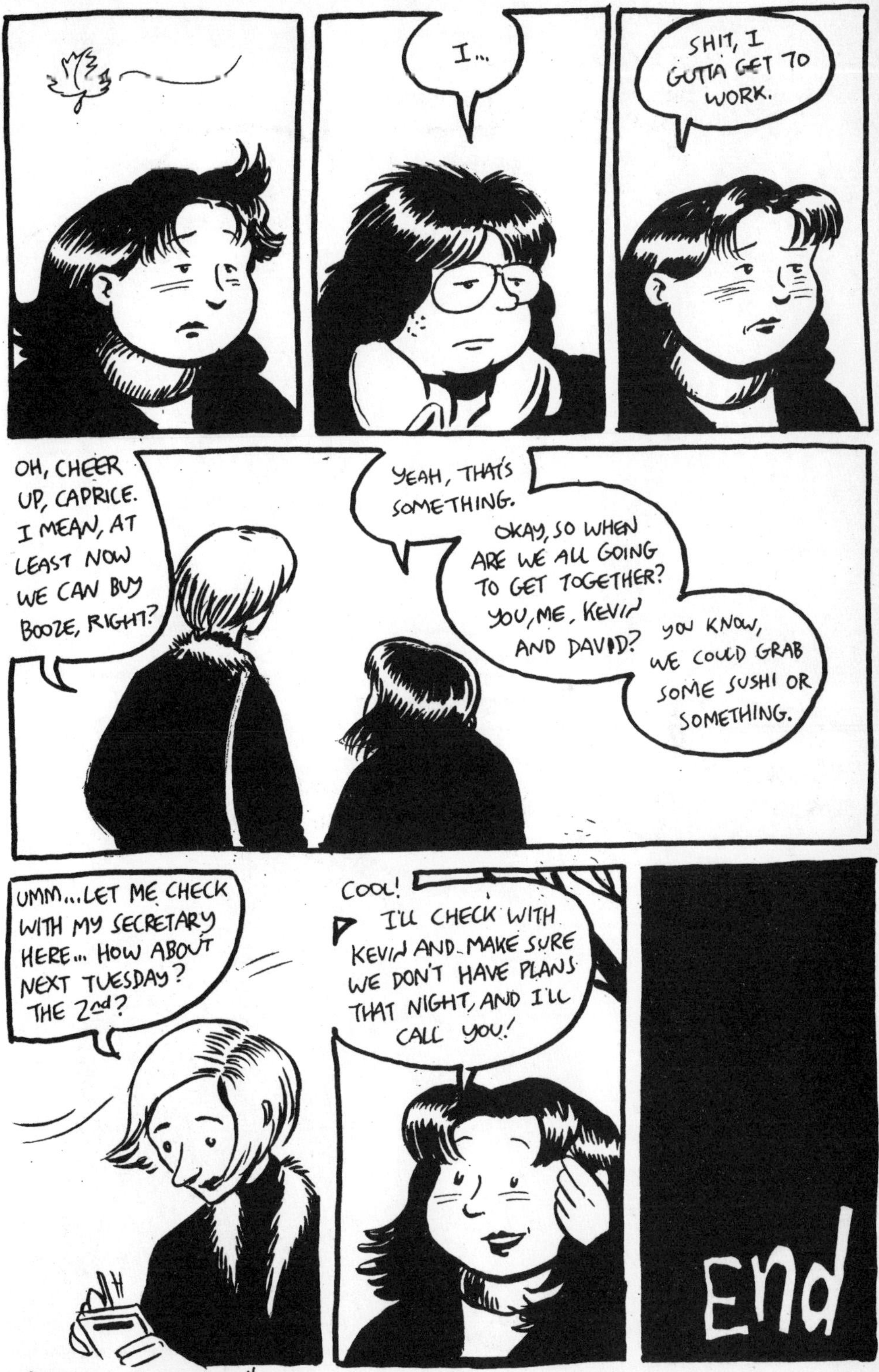
I...
SHIT, I GOTTA GET TO WORK.
OH, CHEER UP, CAPRICE. I MEAN, AT LEAST NOW WE CAN BUY BOOZE, RIGHT?
YEAH, THAT'S SOMETHING.
OKAY, SO WHEN ARE WE ALL GOING TO GET TOGETHER? YOU, ME, KEVIN AND DAVID?
YOU KNOW, WE COULD GRAB SOME SUSHI OR SOMETHING.
UMM...LET ME CHECK WITH MY SECRETARY HERE... HOW ABOUT NEXT TUESDAY? THE 2nd?
COOL!
I'LL CHECK WITH KEVIN AND MAKE SURE WE DON'T HAVE PLANS THAT NIGHT, AND I'LL CALL YOU!
End

9:19 AM--HOME STRETCH!!!

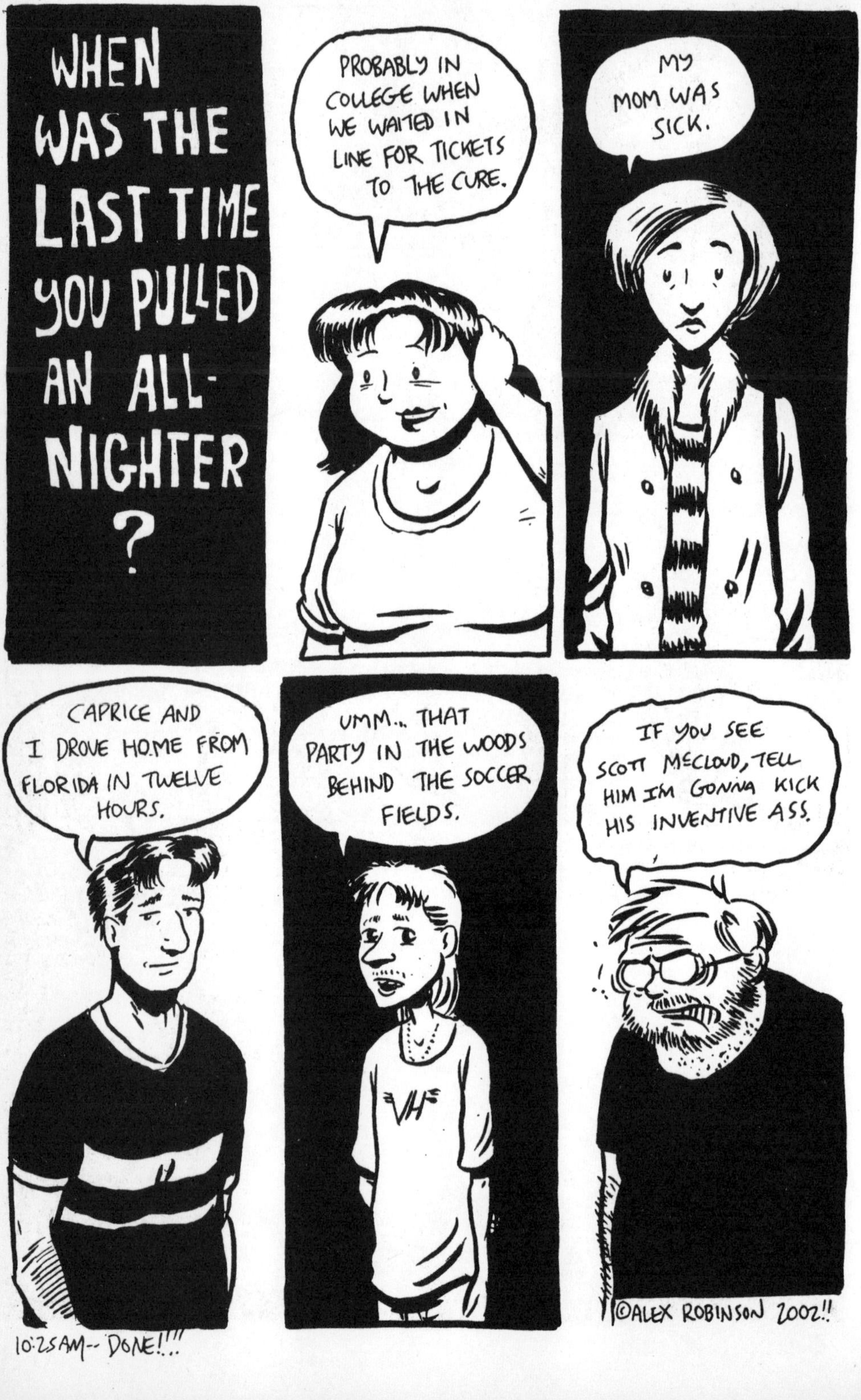
WHEN WAS THE LAST TIME YOU PULLED AN ALL-NIGHTER ?
PROBABLY IN COLLEGE WHEN WE WAITED IN LINE FOR TICKETS TO THE CURE.
MY MOM WAS SICK.
CAPRICE AND I DROVE HOME FROM FLORIDA IN TWELVE HOURS.
UMM... THAT PARTY IN THE WOODS BEHIND THE SOCCER FIELDS.
IF YOU SEE SCOTT McCLOUD, TELL HIM I'M GONNA KICK HIS INVENTIVE ASS.
VH
©ALEX ROBINSON 2002!!
10:25AM-- DONE!!!

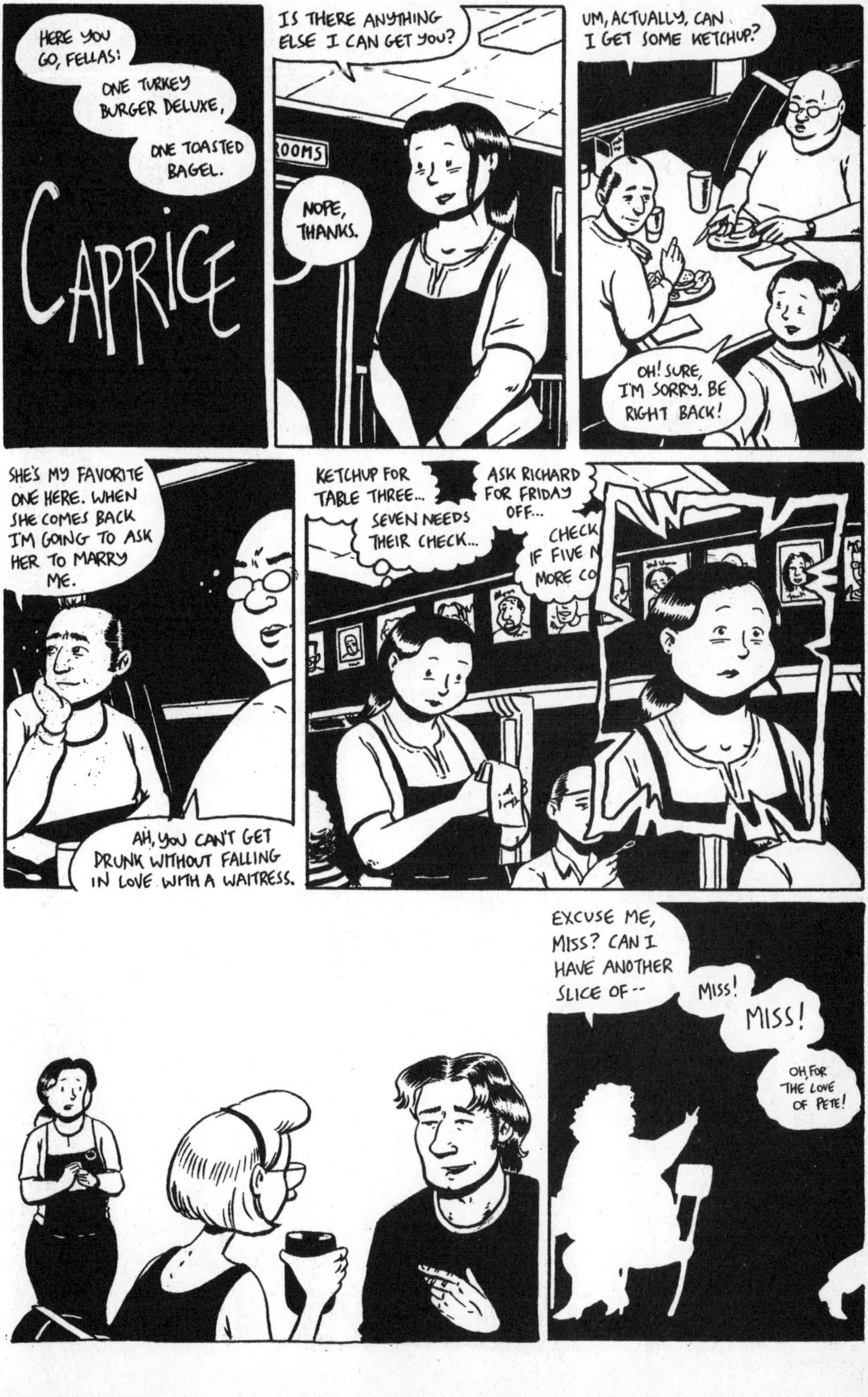
HERE YOU GO, FELLAS!
ONE TURKEY BURGER DELUXE,
ONE TOASTED BAGEL.
CAPRICE
IS THERE ANYTHING ELSE I CAN GET YOU?
NOPE, THANKS.
ROOMS
UM, ACTUALLY, CAN I GET SOME KETCHUP?
OH! SURE, I'M SORRY. BE RIGHT BACK!
SHE'S MY FAVORITE ONE HERE. WHEN SHE COMES BACK I'M GOING TO ASK HER TO MARRY ME.
AH, YOU CAN'T GET DRUNK WITHOUT FALLING IN LOVE WITH A WAITRESS.
KETCHUP FOR TABLE THREE...
SEVEN NEEDS THEIR CHECK...
ASK RICHARD FOR FRIDAY OFF...
CHECK IF FIVE N MORE CO
EXCUSE ME, MISS? CAN I HAVE ANOTHER SLICE OF --
MISS!
MISS!
OH, FOR THE LOVE OF PETE!

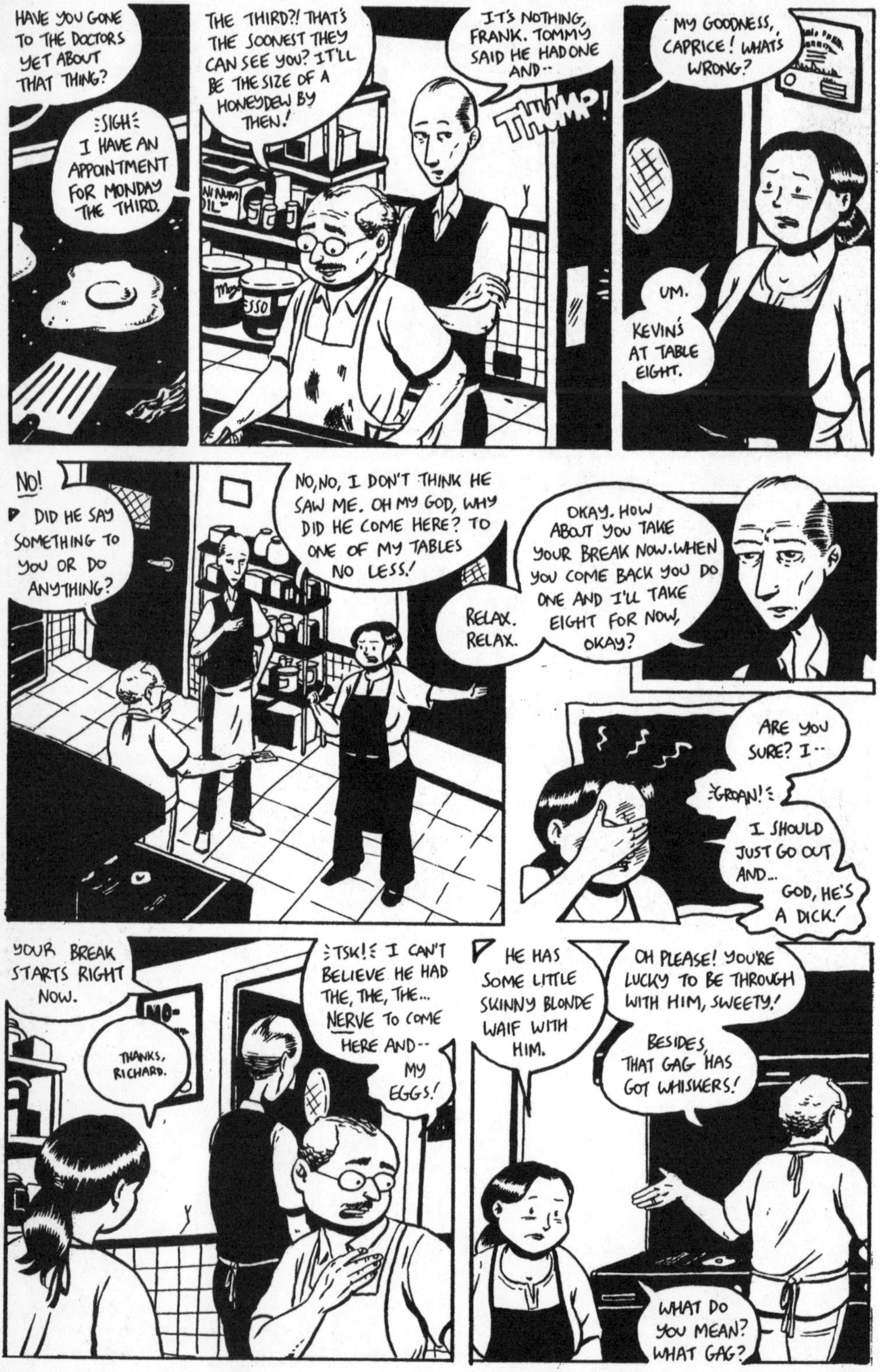
HAVE YOU GONE TO THE DOCTORS YET ABOUT THAT THING?
SIGH I HAVE AN APPOINTMENT FOR MONDAY THE THIRD.
THE THIRD?! THAT'S THE SOONEST THEY CAN SEE YOU? IT'LL BE THE SIZE OF A HONEYDEW BY THEN!
IT'S NOTHING, FRANK. TOMMY SAID HE HAD ONE AND...
THUMP!
MY GOODNESS, CAPRICE! WHATS WRONG?
UM.
KEVIN'S AT TABLE EIGHT.
NO!
DID HE SAY SOMETHING TO YOU OR DO ANYTHING?
NO, NO, I DON'T THINK HE SAW ME. OH MY GOD, WHY DID HE COME HERE? TO ONE OF MY TABLES NO LESS!
RELAX. RELAX.
OKAY. HOW ABOUT YOU TAKE YOUR BREAK NOW. WHEN YOU COME BACK YOU DO ONE AND I'LL TAKE EIGHT FOR NOW, OKAY?
ARE YOU SURE? I...
GROAN!
I SHOULD JUST GO OUT AND... GOD, HE'S A DICK!
YOUR BREAK STARTS RIGHT NOW.
THANKS, RICHARD.
TSK! I CAN'T BELIEVE HE HAD THE, THE, THE... NERVE TO COME HERE AND-- MY EGGS!
HE HAS SOME LITTLE SKINNY BLONDE WAIF WITH HIM.
OH PLEASE! YOU'RE LUCKY TO BE THROUGH WITH HIM, SWEETY!
BESIDES, THAT GAG HAS GOT WHISKERS!
WHAT DO YOU MEAN? WHAT GAG?

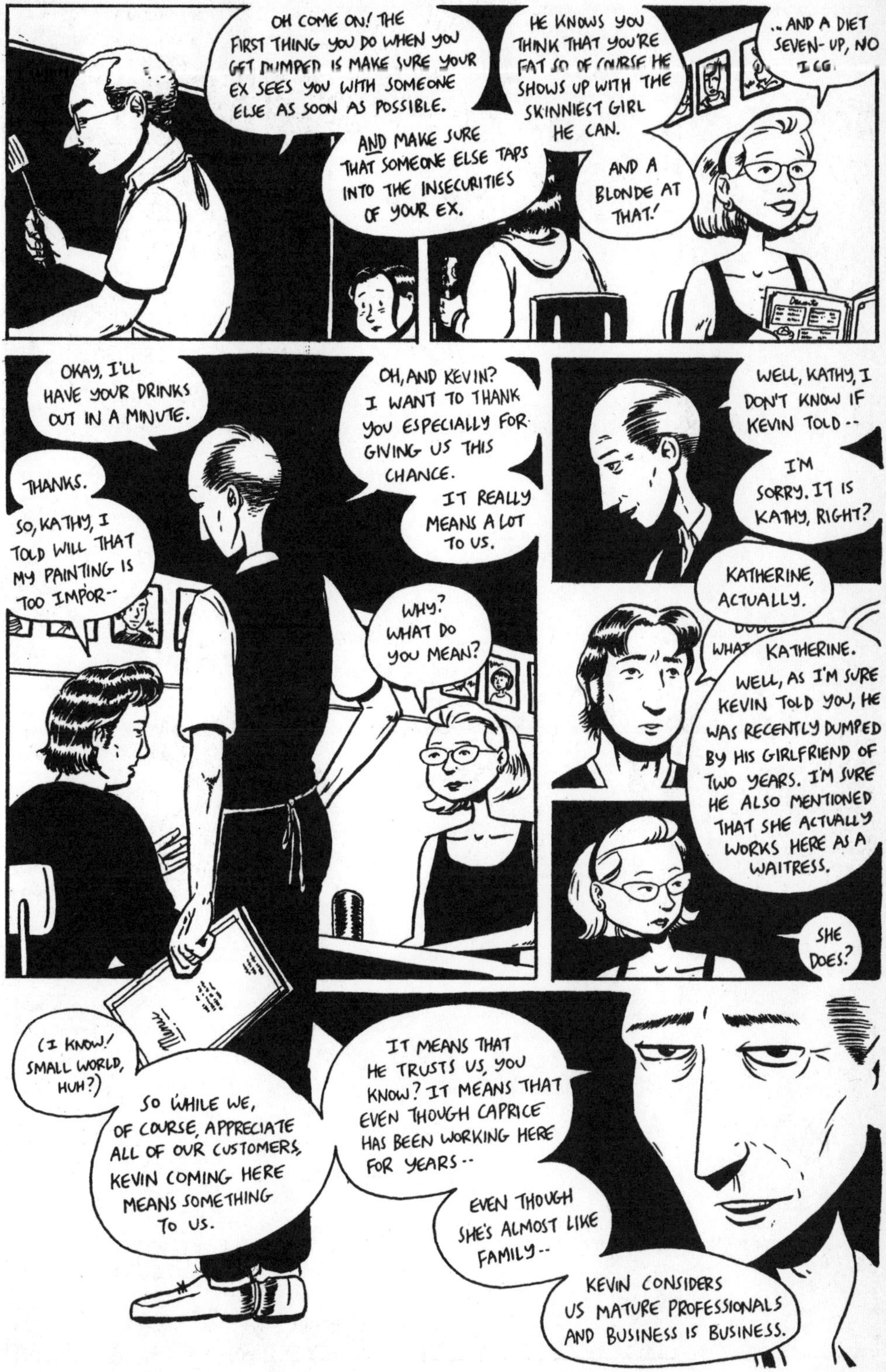
OH COME ON! THE FIRST THING YOU DO WHEN YOU GET DUMPED IS MAKE SURE YOUR EX SEES YOU WITH SOMEONE ELSE AS SOON AS POSSIBLE.
AND MAKE SURE THAT SOMEONE ELSE TAPS INTO THE INSECURITIES OF YOUR EX.
HE KNOWS YOU THINK THAT YOU'RE FAT SO OF COURSE HE SHOWS UP WITH THE SKINNIEST GIRL HE CAN.
AND A BLONDE AT THAT!
..AND A DIET SEVEN-UP, NO ICE.
OKAY, I'LL HAVE YOUR DRINKS OUT IN A MINUTE.
THANKS.
SO, KATHY, I TOLD WILL THAT MY PAINTING IS TOO IMPOR--
OH, AND KEVIN? I WANT TO THANK YOU ESPECIALLY FOR GIVING US THIS CHANCE.
IT REALLY MEANS A LOT TO US.
WHY? WHAT DO YOU MEAN?
WELL, KATHY, I DON'T KNOW IF KEVIN TOLD--
I'M SORRY. IT IS KATHY, RIGHT?
KATHERINE, ACTUALLY.
KATHERINE.
WELL, AS I'M SURE KEVIN TOLD YOU, HE WAS RECENTLY DUMPED BY HIS GIRLFRIEND OF TWO YEARS. I'M SURE HE ALSO MENTIONED THAT SHE ACTUALLY WORKS HERE AS A WAITRESS.
SHE DOES?
(I KNOW! SMALL WORLD, HUH?)
SO WHILE WE, OF COURSE, APPRECIATE ALL OF OUR CUSTOMERS, KEVIN COMING HERE MEANS SOMETHING TO US.
IT MEANS THAT HE TRUSTS US, YOU KNOW? IT MEANS THAT EVEN THOUGH CAPRICE HAS BEEN WORKING HERE FOR YEARS--
EVEN THOUGH SHE'S ALMOST LIKE FAMILY--
KEVIN CONSIDERS US MATURE PROFESSIONALS AND BUSINESS IS BUSINESS.

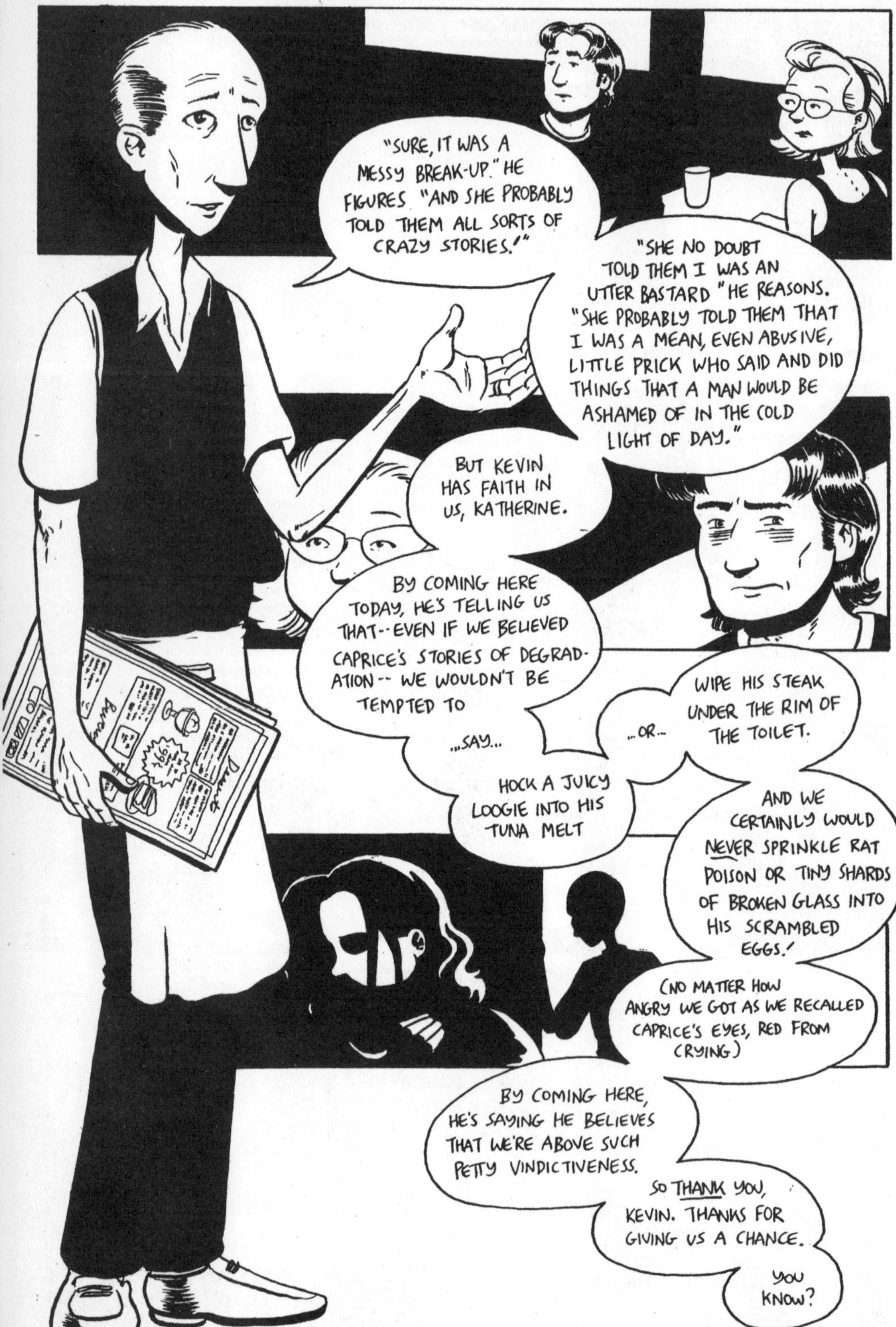
"SURE, IT WAS A MESSY BREAK-UP." HE FIGURES "AND SHE PROBABLY TOLD THEM ALL SORTS OF CRAZY STORIES!"
"SHE NO DOUBT TOLD THEM I WAS AN UTTER BASTARD" HE REASONS. "SHE PROBABLY TOLD THEM THAT I WAS A MEAN, EVEN ABUSIVE, LITTLE PRICK WHO SAID AND DID THINGS THAT A MAN WOULD BE ASHAMED OF IN THE COLD LIGHT OF DAY."
BUT KEVIN HAS FAITH IN US, KATHERINE.
BY COMING HERE TODAY, HE'S TELLING US THAT-- EVEN IF WE BELIEVED CAPRICE'S STORIES OF DEGRADATION-- WE WOULDN'T BE TEMPTED TO
...SAY...
HOCK A JUICY LOOGIE INTO HIS TUNA MELT
...OR...
WIPE HIS STEAK UNDER THE RIM OF THE TOILET.
AND WE CERTAINLY WOULD NEVER SPRINKLE RAT POISON OR TINY SHARDS OF BROKEN GLASS INTO HIS SCRAMBLED EGGS!
(NO MATTER HOW ANGRY WE GOT AS WE RECALLED CAPRICE'S EYES, RED FROM CRYING)
BY COMING HERE, HE'S SAYING HE BELIEVES THAT WE'RE ABOVE SUCH PETTY VINDICTIVENESS.
SO THANK YOU, KEVIN. THANKS FOR GIVING US A CHANCE.
YOU KNOW?

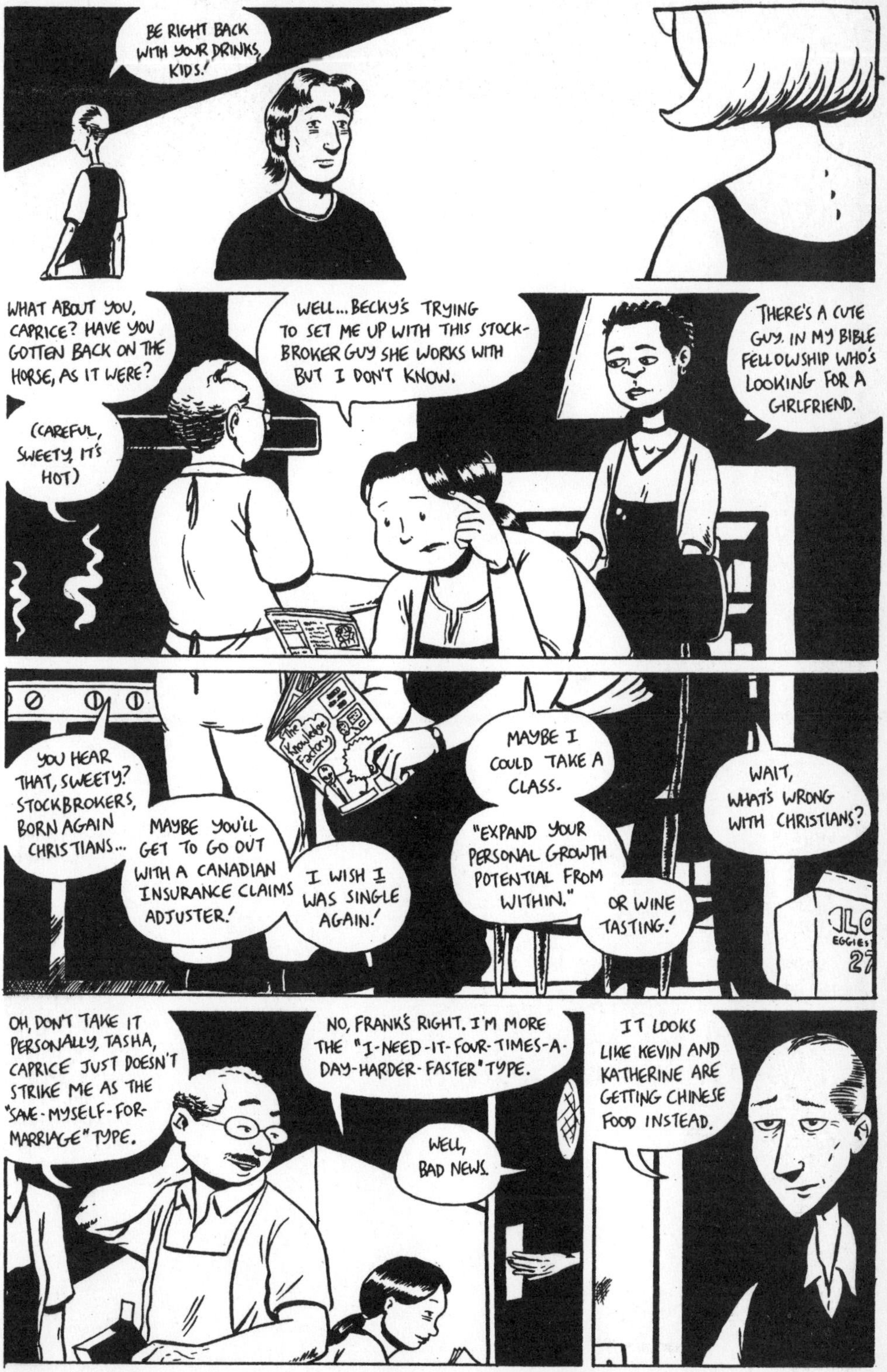
BE RIGHT BACK WITH YOUR DRINKS, KIDS!
WHAT ABOUT YOU, CAPRICE? HAVE YOU GOTTEN BACK ON THE HORSE, AS IT WERE?
(CAREFUL, SWEETY, IT'S HOT)
WELL... BECKY'S TRYING TO SET ME UP WITH THIS STOCK-BROKER GUY SHE WORKS WITH BUT I DON'T KNOW.
THERE'S A CUTE GUY IN MY BIBLE FELLOWSHIP WHO'S LOOKING FOR A GIRLFRIEND.
YOU HEAR THAT, SWEETY? STOCKBROKERS, BORN AGAIN CHRISTIANS...
MAYBE YOU'LL GET TO GO OUT WITH A CANADIAN INSURANCE CLAIMS ADJUSTER!
I WISH I WAS SINGLE AGAIN!
The Knowledge Factory
MAYBE I COULD TAKE A CLASS.
"EXPAND YOUR PERSONAL GROWTH POTENTIAL FROM WITHIN."
OR WINE TASTING!
WAIT, WHAT'S WRONG WITH CHRISTIANS?
OH, DON'T TAKE IT PERSONALLY, TASHA, CAPRICE JUST DOESN'T STRIKE ME AS THE "SAVE-MYSELF-FOR-MARRIAGE" TYPE.
NO, FRANK'S RIGHT. I'M MORE THE "I-NEED-IT-FOUR-TIMES-A-DAY-HARDER-FASTER" TYPE.
WELL, BAD NEWS.
IT LOOKS LIKE KEVIN AND KATHERINE ARE GETTING CHINESE FOOD INSTEAD.

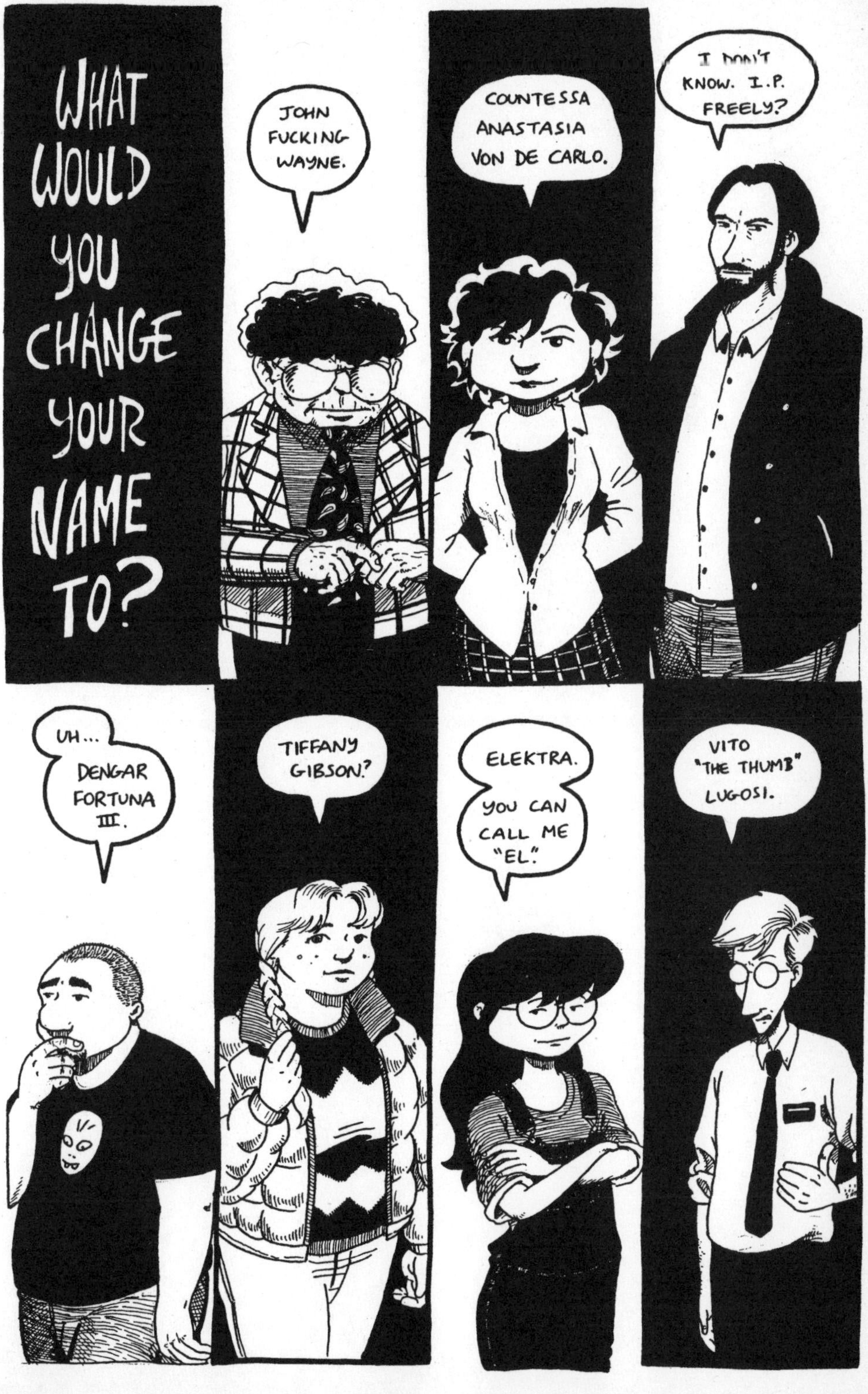
WHAT WOULD YOU CHANGE YOUR NAME TO?
JOHN FUCKING WAYNE.
COUNTESSA ANASTASIA VON DE CARLO.
I DON'T KNOW. I.P. FREELY?
UH... DENGAR FORTUNA III.
TIFFANY GIBSON?
ELEKTRA.
YOU CAN CALL ME "EL."
VITO "THE THUMB" LUGOSI.

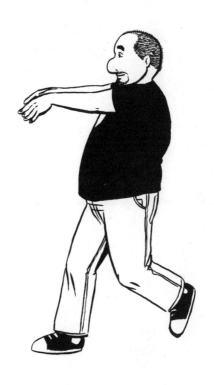